A BRONX TEACHER'S
Travels

GEORGE COLON

This Book is a work of fiction. Names, characters, places, and incidents either are the product of the author's imagination or are used fictitiously. Any resemblance to actual persons, living or dead, events, or locales is entirely coincidental.

Ordering Information:

Prime Seven Media
518 Landmann St.
Tomah City, WI 54660

Printed in the United States of America

"The world is a book.
Those who don't travel read only
the first chapter."

CHAPTER ONE

Saint Augustine of Hippo

I n 1993 I got my very first car, a 1993 Toyota Corolla fresh off the lot, bought only after moving to a two-fare zone with no subway nearby. My driver's license of thirty years I'd used for I.D. and I wasn't mechanically inclined. All that time I rode Bronx buses, Els and subways from the time I paid .15 cents to ride the Number 5 and 2 trains from Longwood to Freeman Avenue to visit cousins.

With the car I broke out of those limits. Went all the way to Maine and Nova Scotia, stopping off in Boston, Plymouth Rock and Salem to visit the Puritan fathers. Then, on my next trips, went south to see all the places read about back in P.S.39 and after. So, I dropped in on America's cradle in old Philadelphia, saw all the Washington D.C. sights. Edgar Allen Poe's tomb, the inner harbor, and Fort McHenry awaited me in Baltimore before Annapolis. In Yorktown, Virginia I saw where Washington took the British surrender. Jamestown. Savannah. Charleston. Made it all the way to St. Augustine, first permanent settlement in the U.S.A. Then I saw Western Europe from London to St. Petersburg. Eastern Europe. Saw Egypt. Israel. Morocco. Got all the way to China.

My Bronx home I's already explored from south to north and east to west on foot. Yes, the Bronx, my borough. *Mi precioso* El Bronx, a beautiful borough maligned by movies and the media. *Fort Apache, the Bronx* thrashes it. They high jack trains and kill people in *The Taking of Pelham, 1,2,3.* And of course Howard Cosell pointed out those tenements on fire during the 1977 World Series. "Yes," he told the nation. "The Bronx is burning." When the cameras panned away from the diamond during the life broadcast from Yankee Stadium, they branded a burnt spot on America's psyche.

It's come back, my borough, though not to the pristine shape that Jonas Bronck found when he landed here on his ship, the *Fire of Troy (De Brand van Trogen),* nearly 400 years ago after a journey of weeks. But new buildings now stand, and the fires are out. He bought it from the Dutch West Indian Company and made a token payment to the Indians. Bronck brought with him a bible and books on agriculture, navigation, the construction of windmills, law and history and a calendar. Fifty volumes in all, some say, though Lloyd Ultan, Bronx historian, says only eleven. Brought building material and skilled men to construct a settlement.

My family brought itself and very few possessions besides the clothes on our back. We arrived over 300 years later in 1953 from Puerto Rico, part of that great post World War II exodus from the sugar cane fields on propeller planes to Idlewild International Airport, later renamed for the dead President Kennedy. Our American Airline flight took eight hours to the American mainland. To *El* Bronx. Manhattan, Brooklyn and Queens, and of course Staten Island, are on islands. We're on the mainland. Of Puerto Rico before that April day, 1953, no remembrance remains. Memory begins with the eight-hour plane ride to New York with my grandmother and aunts. The weeklong voyages in hostile oceans of Jonas Bronck marvel me. I've been on sailboats, though never sailing far, and can only imagine the hardships.

I've been here in the Bronx since, except for college upstate, a short sojourn in the suburbs, and travels abroad. I've ridden every bus and train and have seen it all in the present. But its past now beckoned – and mine - and I explored it in my new car and the next car after that, swerving back and forth across time. By then, I'd put in my thirty years teaching English, Spanish, Science and history in Bronx high schools. With no more lessons to plan or essays to read, I had a pension and I had time.

I followed the foot seps of Jonas Bronk whom tradition makes a Dane from Copenhagen. But Lloyd Ultan, official Bronx historian, told me in a chat before a lecture December 5th, 2009 in City Island library that he was born in Sweden. I'd later go there after first doing Denmark and Norway. with its endless fjords and mountains.

A woman named Ann Hutchinson also came to the Bronx too hears God who inspires her to read the bible and preach. Dreary, intolerant New Englanders people burned women at the stake after the infamous witchcraft hysteria in Salem. In Hawthorne's *Scarlet Letter,* they pin that scarlet A on the unmarried Hester Prynne after a trial where she refuses to name the father of her unborn child. They locked up Ann, too, and put her on trial. She defended herself.

"You have no power over my body, neither can you do me any harm, for I am in the hands of the eternal Jehovah, my Savior.

They spared Ann a burning at the stake, but expelled her from their promised land, driving her not east of Eden, but south of the Massachusetts Bay Colony. "So, it was on to New Netherlands, where the more tolerant Dutch gave her haven in Bronksland, north of Jonas Bronck's Emmaus farm. Many times, I've driven on the highway named for her in our borough.

While assigned administrative duties in the office of the superintendent of Bronx High Schools at Lehman High School on Tremont Avenue, I sometimes ate at the White Castle on Westchester Square. Nearby is a plaque that I stopped to read one day. It commemorates the skirmish between the Westchester Militia and British troops there in 1776. These militia men stopped the British who'd marched across Tremont avenue and perhaps saved the American Revolution.

In 1976. I stumbled upon St. Ann's Church during the great Bicentennial year. As the 200th anniversary of signing of the Declaration of Independence nation generated excitement. A Catholic, I'd attended Pentecostal services with my grandmother. I'd been unofficial Shahbaz goy at a local synagogue and once or twice dropped in to light the place for Jewish neighbors. Romancing a Buddhist woman, I flirted with Nirvana and chanted in front of a G, a sort of Altar. But up to then, I'd never entered Episcopalian Churches.

St. Ann sits on a knoll on E. 141st Street and St. Ann's Avenue, now called La Lupe Way, after the late Cuban singer. But long before Puerto Ricans and Cubans got here, the church has stood since early in the 19th century. It's patron, the Morris family had long resided in the Bronx, and like all people, eventually left it. Arriving from Wales to a plot allotted by the Stuart kings, they purchased additional parcels from Jonas' Bronck's original lands in what's still called Morrisania. Bronze plaques around the iron picket fence protecting its the grassy grounds tell their story.

And in the vaults, that connect to the church lie their remains.

On day, I stopped one day to study the plaques.

Robert Livingston, first governor of New Jersey.

Lewis Morris signer of the Declaration of Independence and one of Washington as general.

And of course, the greatest Morris of them all, Gouverneur Morris, penman of the United States Constitutional convention and the author of its great Preamble.

Representing Pennsylvania at the Constitutional Convention, his great verbal skills helped to smooth differences that separated the delegates. And great writing skills gave shape to the framing of the constitutions wording. His style turned a rough draft into the resounding words "We the people of the United States of America, to form a more perfect Union, do ordain this Constitution ..." He was an outspoken critic of slavery.

Yes, this Bronx boy did all that.

I often visited the home of another Bronx resident, Edgar Allen Poe, who came later in the 19th century.

But it was the Dutch that signed up the young Jonas Bronck.

The Dutch settled Manhattan, New York up to Albany, and the New Jersey coast. Not the Dutch government, but a corporation, the Dutch West Indian Company sent the Englishman, Henry Hudson to also look for a northwest passage to India. Finding sweet, not salty waters narrowed there, he concluded the river didn't lead to open sea. His voyage lays the basis for the Dutch claim to the region first called New Netherlands. His crew became the first Europeans to set foot in the Bronx – in autumn.

In the American Natural History Museum, this future teacher saw Peter Minuet's diorama where this early Dutch governor pays the Indians $24 dollars for Manhattan. Miss Ross, my first-grade teacher at P.S. 39, the Bronx, the class there. The future teacher still hears later Governor Peter Stuyvesant's wooden leg on Wall Street's cobblestones echoing through his earliest remembrances. I still feel the beaver pelts that lured the Dutch here. In Holland, years later, on the way to the German border, windmills blowing in a sweet breeze took me back to his early history textbooks. The blond Dutch girls of long ago on the cover smile through the decades at me. I can taste the fresh milk stored in wooden yokes they pour. I hear their laughter and wooden shoes clacking still through time. And so, my wander lust drove me to want to see where those first Dutch came from.

Puerto Rico is but the preface, the Bronx and the rest of New York are but Chapter One, and as Saint Augustine says, "The world is a book. And those that don't travel read only the first chapter."

So, I go on to the next chapter: the Netherlands - and a young woman by the name of Ann Frank.

CHAPTER TWO

The Ann Frank House (2013)

My wife Martha and I returned to the Netherlands, back to Amsterdam, after nine years. First night there, we took a dinner cruise down the canals, and as the tour guide pointed out the Ann Frank House, I swore I could see through a window Ann writing in her diary up there. "Dear Kitty," I imagine she begins the daily entry, seated in the tiny desk I later saw in the bedroom shared with sister Margot. Did you read her diary in school? I did 52 years ago in junior high school with Miss Dunbar.

But my own journal entry that night began with the rice and spicy beef and pork platter in a rich sauce we ate as we floated down the canals.

"What do the Dutch eat?" Martha had asked before our first visit earlier "Sausages and potatoes like their Germanic cousins across the Rhine," I said. Wrong."

Having ruled a Far East empire, the Dutch let in many flavors and tasted liberally from their East Indies colonies. Visiting a cheese factory, a wooden shoe workshop, a diamond cutting factory and windmills, we saw Rembrandts and Vermeers in the Rijksmuseum, then, half naked whores beckoning from store front windows while I took in a whiff of legal marijuana smoke floating across the red-light district. Skipped the Heineken factory, though I downed more than my share while there. They really do taste better in Amsterdam. We'd see more of Holland, Belgium, Luxembourg, and took a brief foray into Germany. But the Ann Frank House proved the sad highlight of the trip.

The Frank family fled to Amsterdam from their native Frankfurt in 1933 when Hitler came to power, as had fellow Jews centuries earlier from the Spanish Inquisition. So, had Protestant Huguenots from French Catholics and the Pilgrim fathers before setting sail for America, all welcomed as they flowed into Amsterdam, away from intolerance. This immigration let in many of the fine minds that would help create the scientific, artistic and economic revolution that was 17th century Protestant Holland, freed from Spanish rule and Catholic dogma. For like in ancient Athens after the defeat of the Persian menace, when democracy took root, like it did in Holland, an unshackled mind serves as the prime ingredient for a flowering of culture, seasoned with racial and religious tolerance.

They are a welcoming, tolerant people, the Dutch, who defeated the forces of nature as well. While availing themselves of the waters that flow into the city from the North Sea, they've tamed floods but allowed for sea commerce through a system of canals and clever basic science. Then the Germans overran the Netherlands and the rest of Europe in 1940. Though the Dutch have tamed the waters with dams and canals, they couldn't tame German intolerance.

The Franks hid from the Germans in a small three-story apartment house with brown façade, unremarkable next to other charming gabled houses lining canals that curl around the city. Narrow floors of cramped space wait inside, a claustrophobe's worst nightmare, especially when shared with the other Jewish family, the Van Pels, and the selfish dentist Ann complains about, Fritz Peters, all hiding from the Nazis from 1941 to 1944. The tour guide got us in, bypassing the long lines outside. One ascends through tight narrow stairs with the feel of a lighthouse spiral to each small room. I remember the bickering Ann writes about in the diary in this small space. Problems with her Dad, Otto Frank, hassles with her Mom, her sister Margot and of course, those other folks. And there's the never consummated romance with sixteen year old Peter Van Pels.

There's a cramped living room where the two families socialized. The furniture's gone, but I visualized perhaps a simple sofa and some chairs. Perhaps there was a coffee table. Saw the kitchen, now devoid of essentials save the wooden table. I imagined them all gathered for a meal, discussing the latest war news smuggled in, no doubt arguing. The book case is still here, the one that hid the main door from the outside world – and the Germans.

And then there are the heavy black curtains blocking the sun, protection from not only evil Gestapo eyes, but from allied bombers. Poor Ann in one of the many entries displayed around the house complains about wishing for a stroll and fresh air. Saw the bedroom decorated with cut outs of cinema idols from fashion and movie magazines smuggled in by those who hid them from the Nazis and brought them food and essentials. The sisters squabble in another scene my imagination reenacts.

"I'll put Clark Gable here," Margot gets ready to paste the Hollywood star in a prominent place on the wall.

"No Errol Flynn goes there. Put Clark Gable here," she readjusts the pictures. A shared bed rounds out the scene as the sisters bicker about mundane, often silly things, Ann says in the diary, things of sibling rivalry in all places and in all times.

"I finally realized," Ann writes in the diary, "That I must do my schoolwork to keep from being ignorant, to get on in life, to become a journalist, because that's what I want! I know I can write ..., but it remains to be seen whether I really have talent... And if I don't have the talent to write books or newspaper articles, I can always write for myself. But I want to achieve more than that. I can't imagine living like Mother, Mrs. van Daan and all the women who go about their work and are then forgotten. I need to have something besides a husband and children to devote myself to! ..."

"...When I write I can shake off all my cares. My sorrow disappears, my spirits are- revived! But, and that's a big question, will I ever be able to write something great, will I ever become a journalist or a writer?"

"I want to be useful or bring enjoyment to all people, even those I've never met. I want to go on living even after my death! And that's why I'm so grateful to God for having given me this gift, which I can use to develop myself and to express all that's inside me!"

Yes, you did, Ann. You had talent. And yes, you do live on. Your dream came true. It didn't die in that concentration camp with you.

I want to be a famous writer, too.

Her book was number 3 on the all-time bestseller list, the guide says, just below the bible and the IKEA Catalogue, although I'm not sure I believe the latter. After Harry Potter, she's dropped down to #4. Still, she's beaten out Shakespeare, Cervantes, Tolstoy, Goethe and the others. Not bad. Nobody reads my books, which if not dead last, are close to the bottom. Nobody reads me, period, except the few who open my emails these days. But what the hell, I'll write for myself – and read myself, too.

She wanted to do good works and help humanity and leave the world a better place. Didn't get the chance. I did. Incidentally, I was about her age when I read her diary. At least I went on to teach the children of the Bronx and shape their intellects. Taught them to read and to write. Left the world a better place.

I think.

From my third book CHAPTER TWO The Ann Frank House,

It occurred to me while in the house that born in 1929 she'd be the same age as my mother. Mom's still up and kicking at 87, a liberated woman before the term came into vogue, and still doing good works.

The Russian poet Yevgeni Yevtushenko recreates her last moments in his poem "Babi Yar."

They come!" are the last words in her diary. She and Peter attempt a last kiss.

- "No, fear not - those are sounds

  Of spring itself. She's coming soon.

  Quickly, your lips!"

- "They break the door!"

- "No, river ice is breaking..."

So yes, I shed a tear as I left the place and got on the tour bus again. Tears for this beautiful dark-haired girl with the bright eyes and eager face. Yes, beautiful, to this beholder. I might have developed a crush for this girl had we been classmates in school. Only those hard core anti-Semites still with us won't shed tears. Thought about writing a poem, about her and the Jewish people. But no platitudes about humanity's inhumanity came to mind. "Get a whole of yourself," Martha admonishes. "People are staring."

Let them stare. So, these poor words serve as my personal monument to Ann.

Visit the house. Read Ann's diary.

CHAPTER THREE

Belgium (2013)

After the Netherlands and Luxembourg, the wife and I entered Belgium, passing through the bucolic Ardennes Forest, as the German army did to start the summer offensive of 1940 resulting in France's defeat and Western Europe's subjugation. Julius Caesar's Roman legions passed through here, much earlier, to subdue the local Celtic people. And when Rome fell, Germanic hordes followed and later, medieval dukes, Spanish armies, French armies, and Austrian armies marched through for profit and glory. Napoleon's final defeat, at Waterloo, came here in Belgium. As the poet Thomas Gray says, "Paths of Gory lead but to the grave." As Allied forces closed in after D. Day, 1944, the Germans cast the last throw if the dice and once again tried crossing the Ardennes. It didn't work this time. We saw an American tank from the so-called Battle of the Bulge in town of Bastogne, which also has a memorial. The last German attack of WWII was stopped here. American s fallen at the Bulge we'd seen earlier in the American Cemetery in Luxembourg. Then later, we saw Hitler's so-called Atlantic Wall on the north coast facing the ocean.

And so, our tour ended fittingly, through Flanders Field, the final resting place of English soldiers in the first part of World War I. And it struck me passing through the Ardennes that war would be the focus of this narrative. In fairness, war is common to all of humanity in all places, at all times, drenched in us at times sad, bloody history on this globe. And of course, Belgium offers many charms.

Dinant, Bruge, Ghent. And of course, Brussels. A bilingual nation, its French speaking Walloons and Dutch speaking Flemish have coexisted for centuries in relative peace. Like its Dutch -speaking neighbor, it's welcomed religious minorities fleeing persecution. Protestants, Catholics, Jews and Moslems live and have lived in relative harmony – though the contemporary animosity of some Moslem denizens is testing this harmony. It houses many international organizations working for world peace. It has a glorious art, musical and literary heritage. Van Eyck, Reuben, Adolph Sax of Dinant invented the saxophone.

There, in French speaking Dinant, we stopped for lunch on the Meuse River with large cliffs overlooking the town. Its homes appear a mishmash of medieval, renaissance and Gothic. Had an egg and ham salad in one of the quaint, small restaurants along riverside. Martha had an omelet and I ordered omelets for some fellow female travelers in my rusty school French which I lubricated for the occasion. "Et pours Madame, avec jambon et fromage, s'l vous plait." She wanted ham and cheese on hers.

We strolled down riverside, peeking into shops, Martha going into some. "How do you like this on me," she asked about an item of clothing she didn't really need. "Nice," I lied. I did pick up postcards. Skipping the small cathedral, we didn't enter Adolph Sax's house, but the mind's ears heard him playing the instrument that would so shape American jazz. Though crossing the foot bridge across the river to the other side, we didn't scale the cliffs, as Austrian armies once did. My mind's eye saw fiery cannons erupt and angry shells roar from them. And the mind's ears heard those explosions and the screams of disobedient subjugated locals under Habsburg control. Felt the building shake. Heard the splash of their bodies thrown into the river as we cruised the Meuse, got on our bus, and woke up in Bruges.

Bruges, like Dinant, and especially like Amsterdam, enjoys a river flowing through it. Like their Dutch neighbors, Belgians are a welcoming, tolerant people. Like the Dutch, they too defeated the forces of nature as well. While availing themselves of the waters that flow into the city from the North Sea, they've tamed floods but allowed for sea commerce through a system of canals and clever basic science. After breakfast, we took in the sights and walked along the canal heading toward the North Sea. "This water is filthy," Martha exclaimed. It's dirtier than Amsterdam, but entering from the sea, allowed for a great commerce. This trade provided riches that produced great architecture, a variety of Florentine, Venetian and Genoa houses. One housed the Hanseatic League once uniting many commercial cities on the Baltic and North seas.

A statue of the artist Jon Van Eyck greets people entering the central market area. The city brags not only Van Eyck, but Rubens's buxom women, and other grand masters. The church of the Holy Blood is said to house the blood of Jesus, though I can't remember how it got there. After a boat ride through the city we ate a fast lunch at a Burger King. One of many busts stood out, that of Juan de Vives, a Spanish Jewish writer fleeing Spain during the inquisition who here wrote in peace, and befriended Erasmus who also once called Bruges home. Like the poet Longfellow, we too heard the "…Beautiful, wild chimes "peal from the famous belfry. But we heard no canons echoing from the past for wars spared Bruges through the centuries.

Ghent, a short bus ride away, is also steeped in peace. The Treaty of Ghent ended the War of 1812 between a young America and its former master, England. Its name means confluence in the Celtic language and liker Bruges, it's blessed by twin rivers, the Justitiepaleis and Lei Rivers. It also has marvelous architecture and has a famous belfry and. one feels a great hustle and bustle of tourists and people, and commerce. Most notably, Spanish and Holy Roman Emperor Charles V was born here. After his Austrian father Philip, the Handsome died, his mother Princess Joan, daughter of Queen Isabella and King Ferdinand of Spain, of Christopher Columbus fame, went mad. Yes, she was the famous Juana La Loca. Anyway, Charles (Carlos Quinto) grew up here among his German speaking royal relatives in Ghent, then part of the Holy Roman Empire.

In the Church of St. Peter's blood, one finds Reubens' painting of Emperor Charles V, kneeling before a higher clergy man to become Holy Roman Emperor. His armies would pillage and burn, as would those of his sons Philip II, until the two Low Countries would declare and fight for their independence. And earlier Vikings plundered it and others would so later. Though a nice church, as the Brits say, A.B.C. "Another bloody cathedral." I was indifferent. There's a canal, of course, and like Amsterdam and Bruges, Ghent was very much involved in trade. But the towns were already blending into one another- narrow streets with Gothic, Renaissance, and other styles.

But not Brussels. In one of its wide boulevards, just like Paris in many respects, we there found our last hotel. The Grand Plaza is magnificent with its Hotel de Ville, chocolate factories, a wonderful Atomic Park with its Atomium and Chinese Pagodas.

But I keep going back to the Ardennes – and to war - beginning again in little medieval town of Bouillon. But even before, came Gallia Belgica, as the Romans called this region. Julius Caesar mentions the Belgi in his annals. Beginning in 57 BC, he extended Rome's power in what's now Belgium. The people he encountered there were the Belgae, one of the various Celtic tribes of early

Gaul. When Shakespeare recreated his assassination of Caesar in the play with the same name, the name comes up. At Caesar's funeral oration, Mark Anthony says the toga he wore was the same h the e wore during his victory over the Belgi. Latin, then French, became the language of the Walloons. The Germanic Franks defeated the Romans and gave the Flemish people of Flanders their language.

We passed through Orval on our first entering the Ardennes, then through Bouillon, Stopping for a few minutes at its Chateau de Bouillon, so named for its Duke Godefroy de Bouillon. Godefroy led an expedition to the Holy Land on the first Crusade, for a change leading an army out and not into Belgium.

The Duke hocked the castle to raise funds for his adventures, and after, it was fought over by many to gain its strategic position. But we didn't go inside and simply took pictures from afar. Many armies followed. Napoleon was finally stopped in Belgium, at the great Battle of Waterloo, by a coalition of forces led by the English Wellington, seen here next to me. We stopped there also, entering the tourist hall where an effigy of the great British General Wellington, Napoleon's subduer, greeted us. We saw soldiers in period uniforms loading and firing cannons. I studied the battlefield and marveled. And I remembered Thomas Gray, "ELEGY"

WRITTEN IN A COUNTRY CHURCHYARD"

> The boast of heraldry, the pomp of power,
> And all that beauty, all that wealth e'er gave,
> Awaits alike the inevitable hour.
> The paths of glory lead but to the grave.

After Waterloo, the Congress of Vienna gave Belgium a status of neutrality. But in 1914, Germany violated it at the beginning of World War I which wrought great suffering. The French built and manned the great Maginot Line to stop them as World War II began, and thinking the Ardennes impassable for tanks, lightly defended it. But the Germans bypassed the great Maginot line meant to stop them, following almost the same script as in World War I. Alas, war had changed. The Germans learned the lessons of the First World War World War that modern war would not be the static back and forth of the trenches, but a mobile affair facilitated by fast moving tanks, and of course, the air plane. The French did not learn this lesson and were over whelmed when German panzers, after crossing the Ardennes, got all the way to Paris. As Allied forces closed in after D. Day, 1944, the Germans cast the last throw if the dice and once again tried crossing the Ardennes. It didn't work this time. We saw an American tank from the so-called Battle of the Bulge in town of Bastogne, which also has a memorial. The last German attack of WWII was stopped here. American s fallen at the Bulge we'd seen earlier in the American Cemetery in Luxembourg. Then later, we saw Hitler's so-called Atlantic Wall on the north coast facing the ocean.

And finally, Flanders Field, towards the end of the tour, we stopped for the briefest of glimpses and a photo through the tour bus' window. Here rest the English fallen of the earliest battles of world War I, among them including the son of Rudyard Kipling. The English doctor – poet John McRae, who tended the wounded, left this wonderful epitaph…

In Flanders fields the poppies blow
Between the crosses, row on row,
That mark our place; and in the sky
The larks, still bravely singing, fly
Scarce heard amid the guns below.

We are the Dead. Short days ago,
We lived, felt dawn, saw sunset glow,
Loved and were loved, and now we lie,
In Flanders fields.

Take up our quarrel with the foe:
To you from failing hands we throw
The torch; be yours to hold it high.
If ye break faith with us who die
We shall not sleep, though poppies grow
In Flanders fields.

And finally, there's Peter Paul and Mary…

"…Where have all the soldiers gone, long time passing?

Where have all the soldiers gone, long time ago?

Where have all the soldiers gone?

Gone to graveyards, everyone.

Oh, when will they ever learn?

Oh, when will they ever learn?

When indeed.

CHAPTER FOUR

EGYPT (2011)

Land of the Pharaohs
Pondering Immortality

We just I realized a lifelong ambition to visit the Land of the Pharaohs. My trip became a search for an understanding of immortality. Not mine, though I ponder it No, I pondered humanity's refusal to accept death's finality.

After a long plane ride to Cairo with an Amsterdam connection, my wife Martha and I cleared customs, then, fought off the first horde of desperate, pouncing vendors in long robes an d turbans, who like an eleventh plague of Egypt, harassed us throughout our trip.

"Habib, Habib," they yell." Only five Egyptian pounds, "they hawk their wares.

"No, thank you."

"OK, two for 5 Egyptian pounds.

"No."

"Where you from, Habib? Mexico? Turkey? India? Brazil?"

"Puerto Rico."

"Cinco libras, amigo."

"Gracias, no."

Some spoke in Arabic, assuming me Egyptian, and though no one mistook me for Omar Shariff, some noted the resemblance.

Habib, an Arabic word I learned from a poem by the medieval Jewish poet Judah Halevy in advanced Spanish in Dewitt Clinton High School, means friend, or lord. Back in Moslem Spain, for most of 700 years, Jews, Moslems and Christian once coexisted peacefully. Oh, to return to those days! Hebrew and Arabic played an important role in the formative period of Spanish literature. Yes, we learned that stuff back then, in the mid '60's, before the cultural upheaval of the late 1960's, when my Spanish teacher and second father, the late great future chancellor, Nathan Quinones, who gave me my first teaching job at South Bronx High School, taught me the Spanish classics. Oh, to return to *those* days when Giants walked the earth. But I digress.

Nat Quinones lives forever in my heart. Taught me how to teach and I imitated his manner in my own class room. Nat has achieved immortality. Through his students, this retired teacher has too.

Our driver took us to the Meridian Pyramid Hotel in Giza. Though modern Cairo's downtown section, especially Heliopolis, boasts modern, clean, well-kept buildings and streets, the rest of this huge sprawling city of 15 million suffers some of the most dismal slums and poverty I've seen. Leaving the airport on the way to Giza, one is struck by dilapidated buildings, shacks and unpaved streets. It took me back to my humble Puerto Rican origins in and El Fanguito (the Little Mud Hole) in Santurce on the outskirts the San Juan of my infancy, before our island modernized. And to the ransacked buildings of the South Bronx of early manhood that burned down in the late 1960's and early 1970's.

In hectic traffic filled with crazy drivers going every which way, we dodged donkeys, horse drawn carts and yes, camels – and pedestrians crossing streets at will without looking. Though contributing much to civilization, traffic lights have largely eluded Egyptians. That nobody was killed my time there surprised me. I guess with pyramids, mummification, Christianity, then Islam, they take immortality for granted. Bomb sniffing dogs greeted our van at the hotel driveway. One then goes through metal detectors, empty one's pockets, frisked by armed guards who eye one up and down. We normally go for a stroll when hitting a new city, but the armed guards discouraged it, scolding us for talking to a taxi driver outside. We really didn't feel safe walking through Giza at night – despite the tanks stationed in places. With an 18% unemployment rate and a high crime rate, it's not recommended. One no longer trusts policemen, who, demoralized after the January shootings that lost them the people's confidence, don't always protect or fight crime- but contribute to it.

Tourism is down 85%. The hotel felt empty and in the large restaurant, we often ate breakfast and dinner alone. Afraid to wonder Cairo by ourselves or take a taxi taking us who knows where – or for what - we opted the first day for a trip to Alexandria with a guide – just the two of us. Though offering interesting sights, the poverty takes away. Cruise ships don't come, fearing Egyptian troubles and the mess next door in Libya.

World conqueror Alexander the Great commissioned this great city after proclaiming himself Pharaoh and before death conquered him and divided his empire among his generals. Ptolemy got Egypt. His descendants ruled as Pharaohs for centuries in Alexandria their capital until Cleopatra. Then Caesar Augustus came, killing his rival Mark Anthony and Caesarian, Cleopatra' son with Julius Caesar. The Light House, one of the seven wonders of the ancient world long ago disappeared in an earthquake, but I stood on its sight. There's a catacomb, but after Rome, it doesn't impress. Neither does the amphitheater, a small affair indeed after Athens, where in the theater of Dionysus I stood where Sophocles did 2500 years earlier and recited to bewildered tourists the chorus from Shakespeare's *Henry V.*

"Oh, for a Muse of Fire that would ascend the brightest heave of invention,

Princes to act and Monarchs to behold the swelling act…"

Yes, William Shakespeare. Sophocles. Talk about immortality. Poets don't die. We live forever through our words.

Gone is the great library, the repository of ancient learning before the Romans burned it down and the barbarian used remaining texts for firewood and toilet paper – the fate of most Sophocles 100 plays. Only seven survive. A modern monstrosity sits on its sight, though incomplete. Former President Mubarak made off with some of its funds. Had the cross been there, he would've taken the nails, too.

Yes, you want immortality? Conquer an empire and name its capitol after yourself. Yes, Alexander. Even without Alexandria you'd be immortal.

From my 3ʳᵈ book

Pondering Immortality

2011

Next stop, Memphis (ancient Thebes) and its necropolis Saqqara and the first step pyramid, Pharaoh Djoser's tomb. My, what big egos they had. Then I gazed on the Great Pyramids of

Giza, and to paraphrase Napoleon who also came, 50 centuries of history gazed down on me. Magnificent. Overwhelming. Go see them. No extra-terrestrial built them. Human ingenuity did. Egotistical of the Pharaohs, yes. Khufu, Kaphre and Menkaure (the Cheops, Chephren and Mycerinus of the Greek historian Herodotus who also came). But they did create public work jobs for thousands in between the harvests, feeding and providing free health care before Obama.

And yes, if you want immortality, build yourself a giant pyramid to stand for millennia. I climbed a few stones up, but didn't crawl in, which is allowed. Feared getting stuck and my remains not found for two thousand years, No one would mistake for a pharaoh. No immortality to be had.

From the plane south to Luxor, one sees a bleak, lifeless desert. But along the Nile, there is greenery and life. Yes, Herodotus got it right when he called Egypt the "Gift of the Nile." Without the river, there is no Egypt. Boarded our cruise ship and did the temples. In them, gods came alive: Horus, Seth, Ammon, Ra, Amon-Ra. Yes, I said came alive. Osiris especially. He was said to rise every spring with the rising of the Nile. So was the Greek god Dionisius. Could Jesus' rise be tied to them?

And on the stones murals, the Pharaoh, himself a god, pays homage. Got through Karnack, but not the illness that shook me. The 120 degrees? The lamb? The spicy rice? All that humus and other pastes? Whatever did it made me puke all over the ship later. No more rice. Just plain potatoes, grilled fish and chicken after that. Took to bed for a day and missed Luxor temple, but did Hathor, Edfu, Hatshepsut, and other temples too numerous to list. Though Christians hiding from the Romans in these temples defaced some of the images, for the most part they're intact. The Byzantines did no damage and neither did Moslems bringing Islam, nor the Turks. The French and English imperialists did have the bad habit of inscribing their names and one can still see this graffiti.

Valley of the Kings and the tombs was next. Seti, Ramses VI. Forget the others. But not Tutankhamen's, his mummy black and scary after all these millennia, rests peacefully – but not like a god.

And Ramses' giant colossus at Abu Simbel, next to the pyramids, the second most wanted to see place there. The poet Shelley saw it and knocked off some verses:

I met a traveler from an antique land

Who said: "Two vast and trunk less legs of stone

Stand in the desert…Near them on the sand

Half sunk, a shattered visage lies, whose frown

And wrinkled lip, and sneer of cold command,

Tell that its sculptor well those passions read…

"…My name is Ozymandias, king of kings:

Look on my works, ye mighty, and despair!"

They've since dusted off the sand and saved it from the flood waters of the Aswan Dam. Inside the temple one sees murals of Ramses cutting down the Hittite army at the battle of Kadesh and its King Mutawallis on his knees begging for mercy, offering the Pharaoh his daughter in marriage. Ramses took her, adding to his 200 or so wives, although I don't off hand know which of his 160 children she bore him. He liked her so much, he asked for his sister and got her, too.

Me, I can't imagine more than one wife at a time. But that's me.

Sailed south on the Nile on a felucca. The hawker's approach in row boats peddling their ware. Young beggars, too, in flimsy things paddling by hands. One looked at me and sang "Guantanamera" and "Macarena." Gave him 5 Egyptian pounds and he paddled back, happy, singing more loudly still.

Got all the way to Nubia, near the border of Sudan. Stepped on the Saharan Desert sands. Swam in the clean waters of the Nile there. They are filthy black in Cairo. Visited a Nubian Village and walked into one of the houses. The very black owner, who looked like my grandfather, nodded and smoked his water pipe. The women, dressed in the same long robes and headwear they wear in Parkchester, served mint tea. They keep baby crocodiles as pets. Saw two in a tank.

Back in Cairo, visited the Coptic Christian section, where Mary, Joseph and the baby Jesus passed fleeing King Herod. Dropped in on a Coptic mass, but left quickly after quick sign of the cross, always looking over my shoulder. They do kill Christians from time to time.

Did the Egyptian museum and saw those great pieces? And the mummy room, for an extra $20. Worth it. Saw Seti, and Queen Hatshepsut, and her step son Thutmose III who bumped her off, anxious to be king himself., Amenhotep 1- 3.

And of course, Ramses II's mummy. Yes, Ramses of the first line of Exodus: "And then there came to Egypt a pharaoh who knew not joseph." Yes, the same Ramses who dealt with Moses.

"Let my people go."

"No."

Awesome.

Back to modern Egypt.

Just in front of the museum lies Tahir Square. Liberation Square. See the cops kill all those people there on CNN? Hundreds still linger there. We didn't, fearful less something tick them off and they go on an anti-foreign /Christian rampage. Did see them preparing banners for the next demonstration. The protests don't end. They want those cops tried and punished. They want elections sooner than later. Democracy, now. Really, after 5,000years of one guy calling the shots, it's a hard sell. Many expect former President Mubarak's hidden billions to be split among the people. Each person, they hope will get $10,000.

> Beautiful dreamer, on Tahir Square,
>
> starlight and dew drops are waiting for thee...
>
> Beautiful dreamer, wake onto me.
>
> (With apologies to Stephen Foster)

Me, I play Lotto. But that's me.

No. The European banks will keep the money. The military will hold on to power. They're going to kill Mubarak and say he died of natural causes. Then, they're going to stuff him in some tomb in Valley of the Kings, to be, like Tutankhamen, discovered by some future archeologist and his skeleton added to the museum's mummy collection - assuming there's still an Egypt – and a world.

Get there soon. Go during the cooler seasons.

And immortality. Little farther north in ancient Mesopotamia the early Sumerians who established the first great civilization pondered immortality., They told the Epic of the hero Gilgamesh who went on a journey in search of the antidote to death. Didn't find it. Shakespeare's. Hamlet says something about "This too, too solid flesh" melting and resolving itself into a dew. It does. Our physical will be no more.

But there is more to us. I won't burden you with Plato's notions about the real world. I won't discuss physics, chemistry or biology. But yen, here is more. There is something called a soul. I won't burden you here with my Christians upbringing. More in other chapters. But one need not build pyramids, or conquer like Alexander and Napoleon to achieve it. We live forever in the memories of others, through our deeds, through our descendants. And through our writing.

CHAPTER FIVE
China (2014)

Something There is That Doesn't Love a Wall

O ver two centuries ago, Napoleon said: "There lies China, a sleeping giant. Let her sleep, for when she wakes, she will shake the world."

After a long plane ride from Newark Airport with a San Francisco connection, I landed in Beijing with my wife Martha and her two sisters, Rosa and Leonor, who tagged along.

Arriving at the Ritz Carleton hotel in downtown Beijing, it quickly became clear China Has risen from her slumber. Only it didn't feel like China, but Fritz Lang's futuristic 1927 movie, *Metropolis*, purporting to show then how the world would look now. Giant skyscrapers brush again each other and through them cars whiz by on modern highways as if traveling through the sky. These super sky scrapers, like so many Towers of Babel, are not spread out as in New York, but bunched together in this city of 23 million with space at a premium.

I traveled the many millennium of Chinese civilization as far as one can in two and a half weeks. And though I walked a great deal of Chinese history, walking on the Great Wall summed it all up for me.

America, too, is thinking wall to keep out its neighbors from the south. By the end of this century, white Americans, some as anxious as those ancient Chinese with those so called "Barbarians" – anybody who wasn't Chinese on its borders - will constitute the U.S.A.'s minority. "Respect our laws," they cry. "Stay home. Don't take jobs from Americans. Don't use our schools or hospitals. Don't take our welfare." And I couldn't help remembering lines from the poet Robert Frost":

"Something there is that doesn't love a wall

That the frozen –ground –swells under it,

And spills the upper boulders in the sun;

And makes gaps even two can pass abreast…"

(From "Mending Wall")

Ye, the Chinese built a great wall. It kept out other people. But walls also keep out new ideas needed for civilization and culture to flourish. China looked inward. But the Mongols and others broke through and modernity encroached, subjugating for a while a sleeping China.

But before the wall and the past, modernity. First stop? A huge shopping mall across our hotel in the Xi Cheng business district for a meal. One sees Gucci, Rolex, Lewis Vitton. Close your eyes and you think you're in the White Plains Mall or Macy's. China is prosperous and westernized. The wall didn't extend to its shores and so later Europeans showed up at its ports bringing goods and ideas. Capitalism. Communism. After giving up on communism, it's embraced capitalism again, and is prosperous. s just about all former socialist countries except Cuba. No, communism doesn't work. Capitalism, for all its evils does. Human beings, like all animals in the natural world, have a pecking order and classless societies don't exist. Marx said, "From each according to his ability, to each according to his need." But again, human beings strive to better themselves and rise socially and economically – if need be, at others' expense. That's part of nature, too.

We skipped Pizza Hut, MacDonald's and Burger King and studied the menu at a fast food place in Chinese and in English. The Chinese counter girl waited impatiently for our order.

\"Ask what that is," my sister-in- law Rosa pointed to a dish. Even in the states I often must translate for my Ecuadorian in-laws, who after over thirty years living in America have yet to master the English language.

"This is China, remember? I don't speak Chinese; they don't speak English or Spanish." But I read the English menu and pointed. We had a dish of white pepper rice and spicy chicken.

Had a hard time getting my women companions out of there. Happens every time you go into a mall with females. Politically incorrect to say, sexist even, but true nevertheless. We lost Rosa and Leonor and wasted a lot of time looking for them, instead of out exploring Beijing. Found them finally with some purchases of clothing they didn't need.

Next day with our tour group we went to Tiananmen Square where a democracy movement sprung up in 1989. "It's the dawn of a new era," some in the Social Studies Department of the Bronx High School of Science proclaimed. I knew better and so told my students. "There will be a crackdown. Though the Chinese have embraced capitalism, they fear chaos more than anything. After thousands of years of authoritarian rule, there won't be any democracy any time soon." I explained their long cultural memory of the Period of the Warring States (771 – 476 B.C), of the period of the Six Dynasties (221- 589 A.D.) and of bloody inter regnum disorders between dynasties. The tanks rolled soon after, crushing the movement.

It's a huge square crowded with people on a Saturday, some lining up to visit Mao's mausoleum, which we skipped, along with the Chinese Parliament and the National Museum of China. People played soccer and threw Frisbees. Only one picture of the great leader remains, across a street in front of the Forbidden City. Many uses to line the square to see the mausoleum, but fewer do so now. Though still revered, his personality cult is no more. My sisters-in-law filmed everything. "But don't film the soldiers,' I scolded. Li the skinny, be speckled guide with closely cropped hair had warned us not to. They hadn't listened, too busy snapping away to catch images of troops marching in olive and red uniforms.

Across the street, through the Gate of the Heavenly Peace, we entered the Forbidden City, home of the Chinese Emperors for five hundred years up to the 1911 Revolution, but only after a long line and passing through metal detectors (the authorities fear Moslem terrorists from provinces where Islam is still strong). It's a sprawling complex with quaint large pagodas built by the emperors and where they lived in utter splendor with their empresses and concubines and closed to all by high officials. It finally felt like China. A large wall surrounds it and a moat protects it from outsiders. It boasts a magnificent garden. Though built after the Yuan Dynasty of the Mongol rulers, I thought of Coleridge's poem "Kublai Khan"...

In Xanadu did Kubla Khan

A stately pleasure-dome decree:

Where Alph, the sacred river, ran

Through caverns measureless to man

Down to a sunless sea.

So twice five miles of fertile ground

With walls and towers were girdled round;

And there were gardens bright with sinuous rills,

Where blossomed many an incense-bearing tree;

And here were forests ancient as the hills,

Enfolding sunny spots of greenery.

Visiting the splendor of Versailles, I understood intuitively sans history books why there was a French Revolution. "Eat cake," Marie Antoinette brushed off complaining peasants without bread while luxuriating in splendor. Likewise, royalty in the Czars' summer palace outside St. Petersburg and the Hermitage inside the former winter palace, while poor Ivan Ivanovich starved. I knew why there was a Russian revolution. And though the glitter is gone, in the Forbidden City, I knew why there was a Chinese Revolution of 1911.

"During the Cultural Revolution of the 1960's the Red Guards sought to destroy all that was old in Beijing in their notion of perpetual revolution," our tour guide Li explained. Too bad. "The last emperor, Pu Yi was allowed to live there, but was finally forced out in 1924."

Then we took a rickshaw ride in one of the Hutongs, the old neighborhoods of Beijing untouched by the great urban renewal plaguing this ancient city. One goes through narrow alleys and narrow streets, unlike the rest of super sanitized Beijing, pleasantly dirty. As not all Chinese are used to modern plumbing, public restrooms pose a challenge to Western tourists. Calling them latrines bestows too much honor, for they're but holes in the ground. As urinals, they pose no problem for men. For the other necessity – and for women – they're an adventure. Leonor took a selfie squatting down – fully closed of course.

The smell of humanity of the Hutongs and the unpaved streets reminded me of my humble origins in *El Fanguito,* the Little Mud hole in Santurce on the outskirts of Old San Juan where

I was born before Puerto Rico industrialized – and before modern plumbing took hold. The driver doesn't pull the Rickshaw himself on foot as in the old days, but rides on a bike connected to a seat for two. Had lunch in a private home, served by a "typical" Chinese family. The elderly grandmother, friendly and polite, and her daughter-in-law, served us. White rice, vegetables and chicken and, beef and pork. The husband bought our drinks. I tried the Chinese beer. They all bowed at every turn. There was a cute baby. One per couple these days to limit population growth. They dress in modern, western clothes. I would've preferred to see Chinese garb, but these, like pagodas, are a thing of the past.

After a nap back in our luxurious Ritz Carlton Hotel, it was dinner in the *Peking Duck* restaurant, the first of many sumptuous meals with all kinds of dishes served on a Lazy Susan. Beef, Pork, Duck meat balls, vegetables, salad. Lots of dumplings and lots of noodles. No wonton soup, no fried rice, no Chop Suey or egg rolls on the menu. That's all American. But they serve Coke, Pepsi, beer, and an intoxicating wine called fire water I loved.

The next day, it was on to the Great Wall of China, after a long bus ride north of Beijing, to a place called Badalin. Got stuck in traffic. Though not as bad as Cairo, or Rome, traffic is bad. Everybody has a car these days. No more bikes, or at least, very few. Lots of motorcycles weave in and out of traffic. That nobody was killed surprised me. But before you climb the wall and walk with me, a few words about the rest of China – and the man that started the wall. The Emperor Shi Huang Di just north of the great city of Xian.

After a short plane ride, we arrived at the city of Xian, capital of Shaanxi province, and not as huge as Beijing, or later, Shanghai, with a population of only about 8 and a half million or so. A great cultural center, it served as capital of several important dynasties, including the Tang, considered by the Chinese the apex of Chinese civilization. Now at last I felt I was really in China. Though still modern and vibrant, it's preserved a lot of the old, including the Golden Goose Pagoda and a magnificent city wall constructed by the Ming emperors. And though not seedy it's pleasantly dirty in places, unlike the too modern, sanitized Beijing. Former premier Cho en Lai who put an end to the Red Guard's madness in destroying the old probably saved --Xian. Sorry, but I love the old, yet have made my peace with modernity.

Xian has tremendous traffic, like Beijing, and according to Li, our guide, like all China, a crime problem. English language newspaper report rampant corruption. There's a drug problem, as some go to Thailand, bring back heroin, and make a bundle. If caught, though, they face heavy jail time.

There's marijuana When they came to power, the communists shot all the opium smokers to end that problem. They're not as hard now.

We didn't visit the Big Wild Goose Pagoda, built by the Tang emperors who sent the Monk Xuan Zang to India. He brought back Buddhist texts and had the Pagoda built on the site where he was told wild goose would be flying. A good omen. We did pass it and it's a beautiful structure, but visited another Buddhist temple and made offerings of money for good luck. Many people prostrated themselves before the image and clapped their hands.

But the real lure of Xian is that it's the starting point for visiting the Terra Cotta warrior museum north of the city. The emperor Shi Huang Di built himself a tremendous tomb too, like the pharaohs, to ensure his immortality. He placed in it thousands of stone warriors to protect him in the afterlife, each uniquely carved, some on horseback, accoutered in the military outfit of the time, complete with helmets and sword. The emperor had all the workers killed so no one would discover his final resting place. Vanity, all is vanity. He succeeded for two thousand years, but in 1974 farmers digging a well discovered it and it became an archeological sensation and great tourist attraction. The emperor's son, not as fierce a warrior or competent administrator as his sire, continued taxing to death his subjects to maintain a luxurious life style. The people rebelled, as French and Russian peasants, killed him, and brought down the dynasty.

At Bronx Science, I assigned my global students the task of researching one of the Chinese dynasties. We discussed the dynastic cycle, well known by Chinese commentators. It held that a ruling family was founded by a dynamic, strong leader, usually a warrior such as Genghis Khan who conquered China and established the Yuan dynasty. This dynasty reaches an apex, in this case under Kublai Khan. Then, the dynasties become corrupted by wealth and good living and become weak and effective until a new ruling dynasty topples them. And finally, the Great Wall.

After Xian, we boarded a plane to Chongqing – between the Yangtze and Jialing Rivers, though we stayed less than hour there before boarding our cruise ship down the Yangtze. Chongqing is an impressive city with both modern and pagoda like structures. Chiang Kai- Shek's Nationalists capital during World War II, the Japanese never captured it because of its formidable river geography impenetrable to war ships. There, we boarded a cruise ship and went down the Yangtze is the third largest river in the world. The trip proved restful. We enjoyed -the sights of mist enshrouded mountains, limestone cliffs, hillside rice paddies, and fishermen. Barges float up and down its reddish-brown waters loaded down with all manner of cargo Old towns have disappeared due to the building of the

Three Gorges Dam, which we skipped, opting instead to sleep late. We did visit quaint, picturesque stops along the river. At a place called Badong we saw a Tao temple on a hill top, though we didn't climb the strenuous ninety-nine steps up. Few of the locals remain, displaced by the building of the dam. Martha and her sisters bought some Chinese dolls and other trinkets while I nervously looked at my watch, fearing we'd not make it back to the ship. They took picture after picture. "I create pictures with words," I scolded. "Hurry up!"

"One of our pictures is worth a thousand of your words, as these Chinese say," Martha uttered. Wide mouth, I paused and pondered her words. But anxious, I pretended to leave. It hurried them along. We were the last ones on the ship before the gang plank lifted.

At the port of Yichang we got off and got a plane to Shanghai, on the East China Sea, -China's commercial capital rivaling Beijing for industrial output. Larger than Beijing its population stands at 24 million. It too has futuristic skyscrapers and massive traffic jams. The Huangpu River divides the modern Pudong section where we stayed, and the older Bund area where the old European territories once stood. Here on the Bund one finds European buildings put up in the late 19th and early 20th century by those powers that cut up China like a chocolate cake. Shanghai was once called the Whore of the Orient. No more. Past the Bund is a magnificent old section with narrow alleys with a pleasant smell of old. There are teahouses, markets and boutiques. The girls went crazy buying.

And finally, the Great Wall of China, after a long bus ride north of Beijing, - to a place called Badalin. Got stuck in traffic. Though not as bad as Cairo, or Rome, traffic is bad. Everybody has a car these days. No more bikes, or at least, very few. Lots of motorcycles weave in and out of traffic. That nobody was killed surprised me.

We climbed the wall and walked just a bare fraction of it, taking in guard houses, past many tourists crowding around, as my sisters-in-law filmed everything. It stretches from the east all the way to northern Mongolia in the west along China's north. It was built in stages beginning from about the 7th century B.C. all the way to the Ming Dynasty, which built most of it. But it was the first emperor, Qin Shi Huang, or Shi Huang Di who did the main work. Actually, forced labor with great brutality built it to unite his empire. Besides keeping out the so called barbarians, it served as a border control and to regulate trade, especially along the Silk Road. . There are stories of men dropping dead from exhaustion and buried right then and there, becoming part of the wall, which fell into disrepair over time, crumbling in places.

On my first trip to Rome, our guide there pointed out an ancient wall bordering one of its many piazzas in that other city. "The ancients built it to keep out the Germanic barbarians from the north," he explained. The barbarians broke through and Rome fell, neither built nor destroyed in one day. Nothing much remains of that wall except a heap of bricks.

And on the third visit to Germany, I saw the city of Trier where the Romans and as a supply hub for their armies. All that remains is the Poertus Nigris (Black Gate), the entrance to the city, still standing after pounded by Celtic and Germanic tribes and allied bombers during World War II. Barbaric Germanic tribes didn't like Roman walls. Originating in Scandinavia in very ancient times, they descended on the south and east in a mass migration called the Volkerwanderung.

America, too, is thinking wall. But remember.

This Great Wall of China wall stopped the unwanted for a while – but also the new ideas a people need to keep civilization vibrant. Smug in its cultural superiority, China also built a figurative wall and shut itself off from the world and grew stagnant. Mongols breached its literal wall, as did the later Manchu, subjugating for a time this once sleeping giant only now awaking from its long slumber.

"Something there is that doesn't love a wall…

…That the frozen –ground –swells under it,

And spills the upper boulders in the sun;

And makes gaps even two can pass abreast…"

Robert Frost, "Mending Walls"

But most amazing is the old Poertus Nigris (Black Gate), the entrance to the city, still standing after pounded by Celtic and Germanic tribes and allied bombers during World War II. The walls are gone, for as the poet Robert Frost says, "Something there is that doesn't love a wall."

Hunger, desperate poverty, dire necessity, injustice, fear of persecution, a yearning for better things. They don't love a wall. Build it and they'll breach it.

From Shanghai, we flew to Hong Kong. I need a whole book to talk Hong Kong.

So yes, China has risen from her slumber. But will she shake the world in a good way – or a bad way? There are Chinese -American tensions. Copyright and patent. Cyber war. Chinese naval posturing. North Korea. The future of Taiwan remains an issue.

China gave us the wheel barrow. Paper. The compass. Movable type. Great philosophers.

And gunpowder.

War is hell. A war with China would be apocalyptic.

At the end of the movie *Metropolis*, all those super edifices come tumbling down like so many Towers of Babel. I hope Fritz Lang was not so prophetic.

Finally, we caught the tail end of a typhoon in the form of torrential rains as we crossed Victoria Harbor on the ferry for the last time, missed an earthquake somewhere west of there, floods elsewhere, got on our plane, conscious of missiles over Russian airspace which had just downed another Air Malaysia plane, and made it back to Newark Airport.

England
In Search of Shakespeare

England, my England. Yes, I'm, from Puerto Rican from the Bronx – the South Bronx. And though I first searched Spain for my Iberian roots, England played in my imagination and became my second stop in Europe in 2003. My love affair began in P.S. 39 with the 13 colonies, the American Revolution, and mother England. I tasted more of her history in Junior High School 45, then feasted liberally in Dewitt Clinton High School of her history - and her literature. Savored more in college, Chaucer through Dickens, then the moderns in Lehman College. And Shakespeare.

The land of William Shakespeare beckoned. I wanted to see his birth place at Stratford on Avon with the bed he bequeathed to his wife Anne Hathaway. And his tomb. It's a hobby – seeing the graves of famous writers. Took my first sip of the Bard in junior high school but didn't like him, lost in that forest in a *Mid-Summer Night's Dream*. Not a dream but a nightmare of confusing Elizabethan language. Got a better handle on *Romeo and Juliet*, but an unskilled teacher made it hard. Then a master teacher, Mr. Donahoe made *Macbeth* taste better. With another master teacher, Mr. Schwartz, I truly savored Hamlet. Mr. Schwartz taught me the sonnets, too, and I now had a taste for Shakespeare. Served him up to my students at South Bronx High School. Bronx Science and Adlai Stevenson High School. Then, at Lehman College, I read the Comedies and the Histories.

I'd already visited Poe Cottage in the Bronx and his tomb in Baltimore. It's easy taking the #2 Bronx Bus down the Grand Concourse and Kingsbridge to his house, and later in a car down I-95 to his tomb. Getting on a plane to England and then to Stratford on Avon is more involved. I always pay for a tour. Always the Trafalgar Company which takes you places. Leaving your suitcase outside your room, it's picked up and awaits in your next hotel. We took a plane to England and a taxi to our hotel. The outskirts of London look depressingly like New York out of Kennedy or Laguardia Airports But the steering wheel on the right side of the cab tells you're not in New York anymore. Or Kansas. Entering Central London, it felt like dreaming, floating into a black and white movie of the 1940's and 50's – straight through the looking glass that's a TV screen.

We got there three days early. At the hotel, the young Hindu female desk attendant surprised me, but shouldn't have. I know about England's long stay in India and that Indians live in London, as they do in New York, since I first saw Sikh doctors in Lincoln hospital as a boy. But somehow, I expected Jane Eyre, not someone out of Kipling. "Will there be anything else, sir?" she asked politely, handing me our keys. British accent. No trace of Hindi. The hotel was a modest affair. I didn't expect a palace, but for the price, it housed us our first three days. Our stay with the tour would last but one day, before heading to the continent. We wanted to see London and her sites up close. Saw Piccadilly. Parliament. Ten Downing Street. The Tower. Trafalgar Square. And of course, London Bridge on the Thames.

It's impolite going to London and not drop in on the Queen – from the outside, of course. During our first visit, we did the obligatory changing of the guards in front of Buckingham Palace. On our second, we caught a glimpse of Prince Charles going by in his limousine. But not his mom the Queen, Elizabeth II. At Madame Tussaud's Wax Museum, I did wrap my arms around her effigy, getting between it and that of Prince Philip, whose wax figure stands next to her. But at West Minster Abbey, we did see Queen Elizabeth I – in her tomb, of course.

Walked through that hallowed ground and saw everybody. Did the Poet's Corner. Saw Henry V. More of him later. But Elizabeth gave me pause. There she was, the virgin queen herself – and the ghosts of her father Henry VIII and her mother, Ann Boleyn, hovering around. I also felt them in the Tower of London where she lost her life, along with her head. One can't talk of Shakespeare without talking about Elizabeth's reign. Yes, Elizabethan England. That requires a book.

But suffice it here to say that it was a great age – as in ancient Greece. There, the defeat of the Persian invaders in the 400's B.C led the Greeks to believe they could achieve great things and set off a chain of events that created an enduring legacy. Freed from the mental chains of dogma and authority, great philosophers philosophized and created reasoning and ultimately science. The Dutch later defeated their dogmatic Spanish rulers and freed themselves from Catholicism's intellectual stranglehold during the Reformation. And like the ancient Athenians when democracy took hold, the Netherlands experienced a scientific and artistic revolution part and parcel of their geographical expansion, but also of this freedom of thought. Under Elizabeth England, defeating of the Spanish Armada, did wondrous things. Ben Jonson, Edmund Spencer, Christopher Marlowe all wrote in the after math of this great victory.

And Shakespeare.

So, we took a side trip with another tour company before the big tour. Saw Oxford, Warwick Castle and Stonehenge. But the big attraction was Stratford on Avon, in Warwickshire, In the Western Midlands, it's an old market town dating to the middle ages and sits astride the Avon River. It boasts a theater, an imposing medieval clock tower and has nice shops along picturesque Sheep Street. On this first trip I saw Shakespeare's house, an imposing two story Tudor house with two Gables. Triangular windows. And yes, inside, I saw all its trappings, including his bedroom with the bed he left to his wife, as is part of his will.

But most of all, I wanted to see his tomb. I got very angry when it was on to Warwick Castle. I complained to the Tour guide, who soothed me with descriptions of the castle, and as the tour van set out for the castle and I stared down the Avon River A visit to Holy Trinity Church and the tomb was not to be this time. Warwick Castle, stronghold of the York during the War of the Roses was nice. The armor and knight regalia impress. Portraits of English kings by European masters proved stupendous. Saw a rubber image of Princes Diana that floored me. She soothed my anger and took me away from Richard III and the little princes. Richard III, namesake of one of the Bard's plays, is said to have murdered his nephews to jump over them in his quest for the throne, after the death of his brother, Edward V. The Yorks battled the Lancasters during the War of the Roses,

By the way, I did my graduate paper explores Shakespeare's history plays, all save for The Tragedy of King John treating the War of the Roses. *Many Hours into an Hourglass,* examines the Bard's altering of historic time – and events- in order to create a better drama in the history plays. Shakespeare takes the dry, dull chronicles of Elizabethan historians Rafael Holinshed and Edward Hall and transmutes them into art. I try to do the same in my novel *To Kill a President.* Studied Shakespeare with Professor Alice Griffin in Lehman. Warwick was great.

But I wanted to see his tomb. Got so angry, I didn't tip the poor guide. Again, it's the problem with tours. Yet I should have tipped him. There would be other trips and again I'd be back in Stratford on Avon. I later saw Juliet's balcony in Verona. Went to Scotland on my next trip to the British Isles, all the way to Scottish High Lands. Magnificent. Saw Macbeth's Dunsinane Castle, but didn't go inside, nor inside Hamlet's Elsinore Castle as we later crossed the Oresund straits from Denmark to Sweden by ferry. Again, it's the problem with tours. Did walk down the Forum. Taught Shakespeare's *Julius Caesar* in high school. But it's not in the Forum where Caesar is assassinated, but the Piazza Argentina. Shakespeare takes liberties with history. Saw Padua of the *Taming of the Shrew* and the Venice of the *Merchant*...

But finally, I returned to Stratford on Avon on a rainy day. The tour group headed for the house, already seen, so we went instead to the church. And his tomb. Met up with the tour group later. I'd not be denied this time.

The church dates from 1210, built on the site of a Saxon monastery, Stratford's oldest building, it strikes an imposing position on the banks of the River Avon, and has long been England's most visited parish church. Its imposing steeple looks down from an impressive medieval architecture. One enters and sees impressive religious trappings. There's a porch. Chancel seats with religious and mythical carvings. There's a magnificent organ. And of course, the stained-glass windows with saints. But with all due respect to the saints and to Jesus and his mom, it's Shakespeare that I came here for. I could hear imaginary music come magically from a silent organ as I approached his tomb in a chancel.

First, I gazed on his funerary monument, said to be a good likeness. I'd seen it many times in print and finally I could behold it close in his niche, surrounded by angels. Above him two hold up his family coat of arms. And there, head balding, beard and moustache, decked out in a red blouse and black vest of his time, he stands. And yes, he holds up – what else - a feather writing quill in one hand and paper in the other. He was baptized here and is it's said he came here every time he was in town. And here he lies, next to his wife Ann Hathaway and his daughter Susana. Above the grave, a badly eroded stone slab displays his epitaph:

GOOD FRIEND FOR JESUS SAKE FOREBEAR,
TO DIGG THE DVST ENCLOSED HERE.
BLESTE BE Y^E MAN Y^T SPARES THESE STONES,
AND CURSED BE HE Y^T MOVES MY BONES.

I knelt in awe at these words written by, who else, the Bard himself.

Inspiring. I felt his spirit entering mine. No, I'd felt it as I read him, and his words stimulated nine. I made the following poor attempt at an English sonnet.

Sonnet To the Bard of Stratford on Avon

Do I dare disturb the sacred dust here?

Or even more, these holy relic stones?

I merely come your soul to touch, please hear,

(Your words touched mine) and leave alone your bones.

To be or not to be? God let you be

To strut and fret your hour upon life's stage

And sent a muse of fire to inspire thee

You left us with much more than just a page.

Out, out, brief candle? But no, however.

Yours still burns brightly for eternity

You were not of an age, but forever

As wrote Ben Jonson so eloquently

So please hear my tortured rhyme to you Bill,

From one not fit to even fill your quill.

CHAPTER SIX
Finland

That much vaunted educational system

My last years teaching before the joys of retirement, school reform became all the rage. Society came up with all forms of changes meant to improve standards. The so-called Finnish model became all the rage. Among others, educational commentator Diane Ravitch kicked around the idea we should try to emulate it in the states.

Yes, yes, the Finnish model. First, though, a few words about Finland and the Finns. After an overnight ferry from Stockholm back in 2008, the wife and I arrived at the port of Turku, then an hour and a half bus ride took us to Helsinki. One goes miles and miles without seeing people - only an occasional farm house along the way. With 5 and a half million inhabitants (less than the City of New York), in the seventh largest European country in area, this sparsely inhabited land enjoys a low population density that helps the educational system. Helsinki lies on a harbor, with many little boats floating in the Baltic, a beautiful city with many great sites. The composer Sibelius enjoys a tremendous monument in one of its parks. One sees his portrait and a large musical contraption symbolizing his music. Its great hero of the Olympian champion Pablo Nuri's statue can be seen, running for all of eternity in the same park. And most prominent is the equestrian statue of Marshall Mannerheim sitting majestically in the middle of a large Boulevard.

I remember vividly the Russian Orthodox Church and the statue of Czar Alexander II in the town center, in front of all things, the national Finnish Parliament building. Yes, the Russians have been here. I'll jump to the end of this narrative for a minute. After leaving Finland later, we headed for Russia through the Karelian Forest, peaceful and bucolic, its pleasant greenery, trees and tranquility un shattered as it has been at times by innumerable Russo-Finnish wars. In our first stop, Vyborg, a quaint little town now across the now border, we first saw dreary Soviet style apartments in the outskirts of the city that remind one of New York City projects, with less charm, factories in disrepair. They contrast sharply with nice buildings from Finnish days. it's pretty lakes and a renzovated Russian Orthodox Church with characteristic onion dome, brighten up the scene. Two replicas of Viking ships in a small lake steal the scene. Vikings ruled Russia back in the days when the Slavs around the 800's A.D, called on Rurik, Viking leader of North Jutland, to protect them from other invaders. Called the Rus, they stayed, founding the Kievan Dynasty, ruling from the city of Kiev and giving the country its name. Once part of Finland, Vyborg has changed hands frequently these past centuries, like parts of the Karelian. Now the Rus hold sway. Now Peter the Great of Russia rules and gains the upper hand. Now Sweden. The tolerant, forgiving Finns treat well the few remaining Russians in their midst and even educates the children of their former oppressors. They've absorbed the few remaining Swedes who also once conquered and ruled them. And yes, they treat well and educate Gypsies. But these minority populations are miniscule. Like in most of Scandinavian hotels, south American women cleaned our rooms. In Helsinki, it was an Ecuadorian woman from my wife Martha's home city, Guayaquil. Her children were back in Ecuador and, so I didn't find out how an Ecuadorian child adapts to a Finnish school. I know how it works in New York city school. Latin American, African and Muslim kids are good human beings. They don't generally speak English when the show up in my classroom. The Educational observers and higher ups tell me that in 4 years, they need to pass the English Regents Exam – or I'm a bad teacher.

But the Finns don't have to contend with the millions of illegal immigrant children who come across the border daily and show up in our classrooms, often uneducated in their own countries, and of course not speaking English. Neither do the Chinese, the South Koreans, or just about anybody else. Neither do they have a subgroup of once enslaved Blacks never totally integrated into society, whether we now have a black president.

But a few words about the wonderful marketplace by the River (Sea). Tried shark meat. All right, not all that tasty. But those delicious reindeer meatballs are not to be believed. And those reindeer sausages. The northern latitude weather was cool and damp in July, But the people were warm and welcoming, so different from their unsmiling Russian neighbors we met later after crossing Karelia and the Russian border. And the children? Polite and respectful – so unlike from some of the children I taught at the end. adults are a wonderful, welcoming people

Yes, we might learn a thing or two from the Finns. And I'll admit I've not studied the Finnish school model in depth. I will say something about school commentator Diane Ravitch. I read her *The Great School Wars* 40 years ago. Since then, I've heard her moan, groan, rail and bitch about the bureaucracy, my teacher's union and cast a host of invectives against everybody from her Ivory Tower at Columbia University and the Manhattan Institute, or wherever she calls home these days. There, perched on her Mount Olympus, she pontificates, although I don't believe she's ever actually taught in a New York City public school.

But one thing stands out over the years from *The Great School Wars*. She said a School system only reflects the society it seeks to educate. How very true.

Prep schools reflect their affluent students.

Catholic schools reflect their disciplined students from good homes and caring, interested parents. When Catholic school girls get pregnant or when they fight, they're expelled – and go to public schools. We didn't have the luxury of expelling them and sending them to Catholic schools. When we finally understand it's American cultural and social attitudes that are to blame for our educational problems, the real reform can then begin.

CHAPTER SEVEN

Germany

Or, Why Did They Go Down a Dark Path?

We returned to Germany for the fourth time, as the Nuremburg statue once prophesied. "If you rub me, you'll return," the plaque on the pedestal in its plaza promises, though its face lies blurred in my memory. My wife Martha and I rubbed. After visiting the northern Rhine area, and later that North German Plain and the border with Luxembourg, this time we headed south to the mountains of Bavaria and Munich

But first we had seen Cologne on our first trip ten years earlier. There, the Romans established a fortress on the Rhine River. At a fast food German joint, we got big fat frankfurters with mustard and sour kraut and a coke for the wife. "Ein beer, bitte", I ordered a brew, sticking out my thumb, as our Trafalgar guide Simon Nottingham instructed. Wonderful English chap In a tweed jacket and Sherlock Holmes hat who waved his umbrella and shouted "Tally Ho Trafalgar." We always travel with the Trafalgar Company. As we ate, we saw the blackened Gothic Cologne cathedral where World War II bombs fell unexploded. Martha stared at the old church in wonder. 'Divine intervention?

"Good question,' I answered. Had my own questions to ask. "Why did the Germans, the most advanced nation in Europe, go down a dark path? And after many T.V. war movies I heard the rumble of motors above. Then my mind's eyes saw American and British bombers over head, before my mind's ears heard their pay loads exploding in a vision. After Cologne, it was down the Rhine on a cruise on quest for an answer on that first trip. Drinking more beer, we studied castles on its banks, then stopped off at the lovely medieval city of Heidelberg of the Little Prince fame for a lunch of sausages and potatoes and to see its fairy tale Brothers Grim houses. Then Simon lifted his umbrella. "Tally Ho Trafalgar." Time to move on." Magic, all magic – all the way to the poet Heinrich Heine's Lorelei.

I wish I knew the meaning,
A sadness has fallen on me.
The ghost of an ancient legend
That will not let me be.
The air is cool in the twilight
And gently flows the Rhine;
A mountain peak in the setting sun
Catches the faltering shine. -

The Lorelei, a rock on the eastern bank of the Rhine, soars well above the narrowing waterline. Strong currents and rocks below the waterline have caused many an accident. In legend, a feminine water spirit inhabits this rock, popular in folklore, music, art and literature. Its murmur inspired various tales about this enchanting female of the rock that Heinrich Heine, a German Jewish poet, among others, set to verse. As one downs that wonderful German beer and stares hypnotized at the flowing waters of the Rhine, one looks up and sees her. I did. I swear I did. Many a distracted shipman saw the maiden on the cliff combing her golden hair, and heard her song, distracting the shipmen who crashed on the rocks. The German ship of state piloted at times by blind helmsmen have also crashed, after steering the German people towards illusion, disillusion - and near dissolution.

On the second trip to Germany, we landed in Frankfurt; saw the Roman Platz where the Romans also set up shop. Red brick ruins smell of an antiquity that blends with sausages and potatoes on a grill in a cafeteria nearby. Frankfort's a boring city otherwise, a commercial center of banks and finance. But not the rest of Germany. Bratwurst and beer halls. Castles and Churches. Lots of churches. Mountains and loud, cheerful hum pah pah music. Yet the Nazi past lingers and I hear the anguished voices of German militarism's victims and in places see, smell and touch physical remnants of war through the centuries.

And nowhere more than in Berlin, where the wall once stood across the Brandenburg Gate near the Reichstag, the center of government once again after a brief stint in Bonn. The wall is gone, but its surgical removal and subsequent reunification of East and West Germany left a visible scar. The old West Berlin appears clean and well healed. There, in a park west of the Brandenburg Gate Nazi Brown shirts once marched in torchlight parades past monuments to Bismarck, Moltke, and other Prussian heroes of the Franco Prussian War and World War I. Not so the old East Berlin. Check Point Charlie remains east of the old wall, where one crossed legally during the cold war. But gone is Hitler's Bunker, destroyed less it becomes a shrine for Neo Nazism, which still rears its head, quickly decapitated by a modern German society comes to grips with the past and atoning for it. A cruise down the old Spree River, the dirtiest body of water I've ever seen – or smelled –is to float down the failure of Russian industrial waste and sins against the environment – and of communism's failure in general. In places, East Berlin still looks like my South Bronx of the 1970's with it burnt out rubble.

Then, on the third German visit, we saw Trier, on the border with Luxembourg after crossing the Moselle River. Here, Romans established yet another fort against the Germanic barbarians and a supply hub for their armies. I found the customary bare brown brick ruins with the smell of antiquity of all Roman ruins. But most surprising, next to them, a small, yet lively, living city, a picturesque city with a rich history spanning the fall of Rome, the middle ages, and Renaissance, boasting an impressive renaissance palace with a pink façade. There's a basilica that housed the throne of the Emperor Constantine who dropped in for an inspection from time to time after becoming ruler and a Christian. Trier has the usual Roman quarters with the requisite Roman baths. But most amazing is the old Poertus Nigris (Black Gate), the entrance to the city, still standing after pounded by Celtic and Germanic tribes and allied bombers during World War II. The walls are gone, for as the poet Robert Frost says, "Something there is that doesn't love a wall."

Barbaric Germanic tribes didn't like Roman walls.

Originating in Scandinavia in very ancient times, they descended on the south and east in a mass migration called the Volkerwanderung. Though Romans overran Celtic and other lands, Germanic tribes halted their expansion when the famed Germanic warrior Arminius massacred Roman legions at the Teutenburg Forest in 4 A.D. Roman civilization spread through France, Spain and the Low Countries, but not in what became modern Germany and Austria. Could this fact help answer the question of why they'd go on a dark path century later? Yet they weren't pure, shattering the illusion that's Nazi mythology. Non-Germanic people filtered in. After this defeat, Rome merely built strategic fortifications to protect the empire west of the Rhine, but not penetrate it. Julius Caesar distinguishes in his annals Germanic people from the earlier Celts. But their history really begins with the Roman historian Tacitus' De Germania.

Pressured by hunger and by Huns of Attila the Hun, they migrated west and south. Lombards. Ostrogoths. Visigoths. Franks, among many. Roman history ends with these tribes who eventually overran Rome itself. The Franks took Trier from the Romans and into the Holy Roman Empire and Charlemagne sent out missionaries to convert all to Christianity with its blessings and concomitant evils. Saint Simeon's bones are said to lie inside the old gate, relics of the missionary work and conversion. The Middle Ages bring a cathedral and wayward bishops with bad habits. Protestantism comes, for it was here in Germany that Martin Luther revolted against Catholicism.

The Enlightenment came also to Trier and all of Germany, followed by a scientific revolution that brought out the German genius. Guttenberg invents movable print, revolutionizing books and multiplying humanity's knowledge. Roentgen's X Rays. Humboldt's geological insights become ours. Dahlmer and Benz pioneer the car. The museum of science and engineering in Munich displays the fruits of this achievement. Philosophy flourished. Kant. Nietzsche, Schopenhauer. Social commentary. And literature. Heine. Hoffman. Hesse. Remarque. Thomas Mann. And Goethe, the greatest of them all. Social Security. Pensions. Karl Marx was born in Trier, though as it was late, we couldn't visit the house. Martha had an ice cream and shopped for souvenirs and postcards, and I had – what else? Ein beer bitte." We then got back on Trafalgar bus. And, all the while I kept asking, how did this great culture descen-d into blackness?

From my 3rd book

CHAPTER SEVEN - Germany
Or, Why Did They Go Down a Dark Path?

Bavaria on our fourth visit held answers – there where Nazism sprung there, in beautiful Munich with those pretty Brothers Grimm fairy tale houses. Squares. Medieval. Renaissance. Baroque. On the Marienplatz Square with its shops and Victualen Markt fresh produce stimulate the olfactory nerves and taste buds. At the Neusrathaus, or city hall, a glucken spiegel in its tower chimes the time as mechanical figures march in typical, orderly Germanic movement in tune with the music. Germans love a parade. We drove by the lovely English Gardens. Our latest tour guide, Craig Hill from Australia, a jolly fellow, answered many of my questions and offered chocolate and schnapps as he left us in the hotels at night. But not all.

In its beer halls, musicians in long lederhosen socks and short pants held up by colorful suspenders blare out a lively um pah pah music as one clinks large beer mugs. They are festive, happy people. Gone is the beer hall where Adolf Hitler first made a grab for power in the famous Beer Hall Putsch of 1923. It failed and landed Hitler in prison. But he'd triumphed and his followers marched through the streets of Munich and eventually Berlin. That beer hall is gone, destroyed by allied bombers during World War II. In its place stands our modern hotel. But other beer halls survive, the Hofbrauhaus Beer Hall in the old town, where I listened to hum path music and downed two steins of great German beer. It really does taste better in Munich. They are a happy people. But they burned books in their madness. Einstein's books. Hesse's books. Remarque's book. Mann's books.

And, of course Heine's books – as German as German writers are. But Jewish. "A society that burns books will also burn people," he said in the 19th century. But Heine couldn't have imagine how prophetic he was. Yes, they would burn people. Especially Heine's people. And they have lots of pretty churches, these Bavarians. St. Nicholas. St. Michael's. All this religion recalled Mark Twain's quip. "The trouble with Christianity is it ain't never been really practiced." For all its culture, a great civilization can descend into blackness. The churches have memorials to the victims of German inhumanity. But why did they take the path of evil in the first place?

CHAPTER SEVEN
On Germany
Or, Why Did They Go Down a Dark Path?

Bavaria's scenic mountains take one's breath away. And offered answers. The Castle of Mad King Ludwig, Neuschwanstein, rises in the Bavarian Alps like a vision set in heaven, the model for Disneyland's castle. One takes a van up and walks the rest of the way to the castle. Inside, a dreamland awaits. Colorful wall murals depict in the throne room mythic kings and throughout the castle, great warriors finally arrayed, in bright colors. Parsifal. Tristan and Isolde. Sigurd slaying the dragon. King Ludwig's friend the composer Richard Wagner also brings to life these heroes in operas. Christ, Mary, Joseph and the apostles are also here. The king's study. His bedroom. The chapel. And each is lavishly furnished. Ludwig built it not in medieval times but late in the 19ᵗʰ century when it was all passé, the product and fancy of a romantic mind by then out of fashion, untouched by the new realism of his age. The king blew his family fortune on the project – and some of the Bavarian treasury in his vanity. Vanity, all is vanity. They found him floating dead in a lake one day. The official version says accident. Murder? More probable as the parliament no doubt decided enough was enough. German leaders have also shared this sense of grandeur and illusion. Bismarck. The Kaiser. And Adolph Hitler. All is vanity.

And then there's Dachau Concentration Camp on the outskirts. Not as bleak as Auschwitz in Poland which I also saw. Didn't see the shoes and hair of Jews that nearly made me puke. Dachau was a transition camp and besides Jews, held political but there's the shooting wall and a trench that collected the blood of the executed in front of a metal fence surrounding the complex. Guard towers. Bunk houses where the victims worked to death ate meager rations and slept. And a crematorium where the dead were burned. Couldn't quite savor the roast duck later at a fancy Munich restaurant.

And I remembered a letter in Barbara Tuchman's *The Guns of August* written by French writers to their German counterparts after the German invasion of Belgium in undeclared war and the destruction of Louvain and the great medieval library at the beginning of World War It asks, "Are you the descendants of Goethe, or of Attila the Hun?" And there's Spencer Tracy in the movie "Judgment at Nuremburg. A judge prosecuting war criminal, he observes a festive celebration of German musicians in lederhosen and shorts drinking and dancing... Before rendering a verdict, he comments on the crimes against humanity." Can't tell whether this was all done by the German people or by Genghis Khan and his Mongol hordes that just passed through here."

The Versailles Treaty ending World War I exacted great misery on Germany. War reparations reduced boarders. Demilitarization. Political chaos. And a staggering inflation that devalued the German mark to an incredible level. Many a German lamented with Heinrich Heine...

"A sadness has fallen on me."

It led to search for a savior – a superman – a German mythological hero like Parsifal or Siegfried - and for scapegoats to explain the misery. Adolf Hitler then appeared, a knight in Nazi regalia, as often depicted in propaganda posters.

A great civilization can descend into madness during times of social economic and political stress – including ours. German armies conquered an area about as wide as ancient Romans. Scandinavia in the north, to the Pyrenees in the south and almost to the pyramids of Egypt and east to the Gates of Moscow. But at the end, it led them down a dark road not unlike an end of times, like in a Wagner opera. Germanic Norse myths prophesy it all in the Norse classic, the Great *Edda*…'

> The sun turns black, earth sinks to the sea
> The hot stars fall from the sky
> And fire leaps high above heaven itself.

Those allied bombers rain the fire from the sky. Then the fat lady sang. But Germans have come to grips with a past they acknowledge and atone for. Their churches display memorials to the victims. Even Dachau now has a synagogue. The German economic and industrial giant helps other nations. For the *Great Edda* also prophesizes a new heaven and a new earth…

> In wondrous beauty once again.
> The dwelling roofed with gold
> The fields unsowed bear ripened fruit.
> In happiness forevermore.

The evil is in us all. Yes, the devil is inside us all. The Turks and the million Armenian Christians they massacred. Rwanda. The killing fields of Cambodia. Serbian ethnic cleansing. Great civilization can descend into madness.

So, can ours, as the poet Louis Ginsburg says in his "Atomic":

> The splitting apart
> Of man from man
> Dooms more than splitting
> The atom can.

> In one blaze, will
> All things be gone:
> The Empire State
> And the Parthenon.

And must the sudden

Atom's flash

Turn cities, statues,

And poem's to ash?

Quick! The foe

In us is curled,

More fearsome than any

Foe in the world

CHAPTER EIGHT

Greece

In the Foot Steps of Oedipus the King

THE isles of Greece! The isles of Greece!

Where burning Sappho loved and sung,

Where grew the arts of war and peace,

Where Delos rose, and Phoebus sprung!

Eternal summer gilds them yet,

But all, except their sun, is set.

I placed these lines from a Lord Byron poem on a bulletin board when I first taught Greek mythology in South Bronx High School in the fall of 1982. That year I also taught the play *Oedipus the King* by Sophocles and introduced my students to the concept of fate vs. free will. Though I'd not yet been to Greece, I recreated the Parthenon on a bulletin board, placing this prototype of Western architecture in the center, peopled by resurrected gods on Mount Olympus and Greek heroes here on earth.

A painting of the Oracle of Delphi occupied its own space on a separate wall, hot fumes from its spring steaming out.

On yet another wall I placed a drawing of the Theater of Dionysus.

I eventually got to Greece over twenty years later, and arriving with my wife Martha in Athens, on the taxi ride to the hotel marveled how this Mediterranean climate and tropical trees reminded me of my native Puerto Rico. My trip became in part a quest in the footsteps of Oedipus the King. My first stop was Theater of Dionysus.

The play *Oedipus Tyrannous*, or *Oedipus Rex*, was first performed there and it still stands after 2,500 years, in the shadow of the Acropolis and the Parthenon. In this stone amphitheater with horseshoe shape, in an ancient springtime long ago, Athenians celebrated the wine harvest and the rebirth of the god Dionysus, who died and resurrected with the grape vines every year. Antiquity's great playwrights performed their tragedies and comedies, competing for prizes. I stood, humbled on its stage and faced an imaginary ancient Athenian audience resting on cushions against its stone seats, awaiting my performance. The great Sophocles stands in the arena shouting stage directions. Switch to the present and other lovers of theater and would be thespians gather around, assuming I'd recite lines from the golden age of Spanish theater.

"Will you do Lope de Vega?"

" Calderon de la Barca?

"Tirso de Molina?"

"No Shakespeare," I surprised them, and go on to recite to these bewildered tourists the chorus from Shakespeare's *Henry V.*

"Oh, for a Muse of Fire that would ascend the brightest heaven of invention,

A Kingdom for stage

Princes to act

And Monarchs to behold the swelling act..."

Totally blew their minds.

After wards, we took in some of the other sights and next day, picked up the tour. With our guide we trekked up the long, arduous path to the Acropolis – the high place – a hilly outcropping of rock that's the cultural center of Athens. No, of Greece. No of Western civilization. Here, Socrates stopped passersby to ask question of ethics and politics before annoyed Athenians put him to death for dissing the Greek gods and "corrupting" the minds of the young. Here, Plato took notes as Socrates spoke and his greatest pupil Aristotle also walked, leaving western civilization his legacy. Once we caught our breath, we marveled at the great classical ruins of temples and buildings, and gazed on the Parthenon, temple of the goddess, Athena divine mother of ancient Athens, and its magnificent Doric columns topped at either end by triangular pediments that once boasted sculpture.

We did other towns and cities traveling through mountainous terrain. Except for certain lovely spots, the Greek country is rocky and not particularly pretty. Eleusis. Olympia. Kalambaca. Marathon. Thermopylae.

But this trip became all about Oedipus, Corinth, Thebes and the Delphic oracle. And about our destiny in life and is it fate or free will.

We didn't get to Oedipus's birthplace of Thebes, where the main drama takes place. "There are no ruins there," our tour guide disappointed. Oedipus' father the Theban King Laius visits the Delphic Oracle where he learns his newborn son will kill him and marry his wife, Oedipus' mother, Jocasta. He commands the baby be killed, but a shepherd takes pity and takes him to Corinth, where King Polybus and his queen Merope, adopt him, and where he grows up.

Corinth was one of the great city states of ancient Greece. It's on the Isthmus of Corinth that joins the Peloponnesus to mainland Greece, halfway between Sparta and Athens and its long past goes back to Neolithic times. Playing an important role in Greek mythology, it's the stage for much history from classical times, through the Hellenistic period after Alexander the Great conquered it, past Roman and later Byzantine times and later Turkish rule. It boasts some marvelous remains. Here Jason of the Argonaut wronged his sorceress wife Medea, but she won the day, as the playwright Euripides tells in his great tragedy of the same name. Saint Paul preached here and later wrote his Letter to the Corinthians. We stood on the very spot where he was run out of town.

But above all, it's where Oedipus grows up.

On arriving in Corinth, one first sees the canal. Started many times, including an attempt by the Roman Emperor Nero, it wasn't finished until 19th century. We saw bungee jumpers dipping into the canal and boats crossing the Peloponnese's waters. The modern town, though quaint, only offered coffee and a role after the trip from Athens. It's the ancient ruins that impress. Apollo has a temple here with Corinthian columns. The ancient Romans built a fountain. Its ancient stones took me back to Oedipus, who like many Greeks visited the oracle of Apollo at Delphi.

Delphi lies in upper central Greece, along the slope of Mount Parnassus. Ancient Greeks thought it the center of the world. It was truly Apollo's city and his temple's columns still stand, and here, he defeated the Python serpent. Delphi was the precursor to the Olympic Games and held the Athenian Treasury in a temple still standing. We visited the museum, which holds great treasures itself, including the sword of Miltiades, master of the Athenian defeat of Persia at the Battle of Marathon. Though flash photography is forbidden, I couldn't resist and took a picture when the guards weren't looking. But the main draw was the Oracle where people of all walks and class came to divine their destiny's. Later, the Byzantine emperor Theodosius I closed it and later Christian zealots destroyed much of its temple and statues as blasphemous paganism.

But in its heydays people came. Breathing in hot fumes from a spring, the Pythia, or diviner, went into a trance and uttered ravings interpreted by a priest of Apollo. A Pythia would tell Oedipus, like one told his biological father King Laius, that Oedipus would kill his father and marry his mother.

Before starting the play, I tackled the subject of fate vs. free will by telling my students the tale of three childhood friends. One, X, lived in a dilapidated apartment, and came from the poorest of the poor – a family of seven children. The two others, Y and Z, brothers, lived downstairs in a beautifully furnished apartment, raised by more affluent parents

"So, who succeeded in life? X with his good grades got a scholarship to Philips Andover Academy, went on to Harvard and later became the Commissioner of Social Services in Bridgeport, Connecticut. Y became a big-time drug dealer and at first made a lot of. money. Later, busted by an undercover DEA agent, Y went to jail for a few years and when he got out, was gunned down in front of a more spacious home he later bought for his mother. His brother Z became a heroin addict and later died of AIDS. So, who or what decided their fate?".

"They had a choice in life and chose their own," the clear majority voted for free will.

I pushed the social scientist position that environment plays a role, explaining that in those days, our South Bronx Hunts Point section had the highest density of drug addicts in the world – after the communists shot all the opium smokers in China. I added that Y and Z' materialistic parent's values played a role, as they loved fine things. **White** Puerto Ricans they were snobbish and looked down on their poorer, darker neighbors. X's parents had different values. I threw in genetics, as our genes play a role.

"So? Who or what determined their destiny in life?" Some said God, some our stars.

A Black female voice that echoes through three decades spoke for the majority. "They knew what they were doing. You have got to pay the price."

So, which is it?

We read the play.

Shocked at hearing his destiny, Oedipus, thinking Polybius and Meriope of Corinth, his adopted parents, his biological parents, runs away. At a crossroad, he comes across an old man he kills in a case of road rage over who shall pass first. He continues to Thebes where he become king – and marries – who else? The recently widowed Queen Jocasta of the slain King. Years later, there is famine and death and Oedipus summons the great Seer Tiresias who informs Oedipus the gods are angry because the murderer of King Laius is still in Thebes. The outraged Oedipus orders the man found and banished, not knowing of course he's condemning himself.

The plot unravels, and Oedipus realizes at the end he is the wanted man and banishes himself – after gauging out his eyes that has seen his perversion. Now he finally sees the truth. All along I pointed out the dramatic ironies. My students saw the greatest irony of all – that Oedipus in trying to run away from his fate, ends running right into it at the crossroads where he kills King Laius, his father, unbeknown to him. Gave them a little of Aristotle's *Poetics* in which the philosopher cites Oedipus as the best example of the perfect tragedy. Even gave them a taste of The *Interpretation of Dreams* where Freud touches on the Oedipal Complex.

And at the end, I'd tell them the conclusion I reached - that life is like an ocean on which we find ourselves on a row boat with a paddle. "We don't decide to be here, nor how we get here, but must choose which way to steer the boat."

Finally, from Athen's great port of Piraeus, it was off to Turkey and other Greek Isles.

Note: I tell the story of these two ill-fated friends who nearly took me with them to an early grave in my unpublished memoir, *A Bronx Teacher Saga*. An adapted piece, "On a Bronx Roof Top Long Ago," appears in the recently released *Bronx Memoir Project*, Bronx Council on the Arts, Charlie Vazquez, Editor, 2014, 17-19. If you haven't tired of my prose after this second booth, I'll send you a copy on request.

CHAPTER NINE

Italy

The Search for the Jesus of my Youth

All roads lead to Rome – and just about all airlines fly there too. I forgot which one we took to the eternal city – but not the hassles finding transportation to our hotel, though we finally got a mini bus that took us there. Forget the name of the hotel, too, but not the first set of ruins we saw as we neared it. "What are those?" I asked the driver in English, not yet ready to try my Pimsleur's *Italian in Ten Days*. The brown stones and rocks speak though, still standing after many centuries, though many are gone.

"The Baths of Caracalla," he said.

The ancient Romans loved their baths and I'd already been to Bath, England and would later see another in Trier Germany. They brought in water from aqueducts, like the one the emperor Claudius built, and like the one I saw in Segovia, Spain. If you didn't know, the ancient Romans were great engineers. Checking into the hotel, we unpacked quickly and headed straight for the Forum, just a couple of blocks away, passing the emperor Nero's home, the Domo Aurea, saved for another day.

A scent of antiquity pervades the Forum, a smell of old brick and stone time never dissipated. Not the Dark ages, not the Renaissance or Baroque periods, nor everything that followed. The emperors are still here in the monuments their egos erected.

Trajan's raises a salute from his statue, which a future would be emperor, Benito Mussolini, imitates in later newsreels. Marcus Aurelia on horseback guards the Piazza del Campidoglio, though in a much later rendition by Michelangelo. Gold will cover the emperor's equestrian statue, it's said – just before the end of the world. In the meantime, the Capitoline museum holds more emperors, philosophers, and Renaissance people.

A scent of religion also pervades this spot, once the center of the known world. My journey to Italy became a sort of religious quest for Jesus and an examination of my own religious beliefs. In the old Mamertine Prison (*Carcere Mamertino*) St. Paul himself languished, managing a few miracles. We'd follow his foots steps on later trips. We've not been to Damascus Syria – and don't plan to get there anytime soon - or the road where he had his conversion.

It's said a sudden a light from heaven flashed around him and he fell to the ground and heard a voice. "Saul, Saul, why do you persecute me?" "Who are you, Lord?" Saul asked. "I am Jesus, whom you are persecuting," he replied. "Now get up and go into the city, and you will be told what you must do." Saul, now Paul, had to convert Jews and gentiles alike. We've been to Ephesus in Turkey and to Corinth where he avoided jail. But the Romans finally got him. My wife Martha got very emotional in the church that now stands on the spot and prayed and made a few signs of the cross.

My own views of religion have evolved.

We came around, back to the forum, past the temple of the Vestal Virgins, and had a quick sandwich. Ham and Cheese on Italian bread from a vendor for too many Euros. They've lost respect for American money these Europeans – all before the economic crisis and the decline of the Euro.

Then, we entered the ruins of the Coliseum, begun by Vespasian and finished by his son Titus to win the adoration of the people. Yes, it really looks like the old Yankee stadium and took our breath away. But it's not Babe Ruth inside or the Bronx Bombers. Closed my eyes. No more ruins, but a vibrant arena. I see those poor gladiators fighting for their lives. Hear the cheers of the frenzied mob enjoying a day of bread and circuses provided by Roman emperors eager to please it and stay in power. A victorious gladiator stands over his vanquished opponent, awaiting the emperor's signal. Thumbs down! Off with the poor victim's head, held up to the mob that goes wild. I smell the water filling it to reenact the mock sea battles of antiquity, and again hear the mob cheer the gore and violence. We see those lions going berserk and tearing up the early Christians. The mob goes berserk, too.

And from the second deck, I study Constantine's column in front of the Coliseum commemorating this Roman general and future emperor's victory over a rival general whom he defeated. There on the column is the cross in the sky it's said he took as an omen to convert to Christianity. Constantine won, became emperor and made Christianity the state religion. Soon everybody had to become a Christian whether he or she wanted to or not. Later, the Merovingian Frankish kings force the Germanic tribes that brought down the Roman Empire to also become Christians, beheading all clinging to the old Germanic gods. Queen Isabella likewise said all the Indians and African slaves of the new world needed to convert – or else.

These are the roots of my own Christian upbringing.

My mother never went to church, a limited word robe causing this dereliction of faith. She feared more the contemptuous stares of better-heeled parishioners than God's wrath, though later discovered Him again when her wardrobe improved. She did send me to St. Athanasius once a week for religious instruction for my first communion and confirmation.

At Saint Athanasius fifty years ago, a nun dressed in black, a bonnet on her head, takes the eraser and dusts out a white, round circle on the blackboard. "This is your soul at birth, pure and clean," the good sister explains "Well, not exactly," she continues," because we inherited Adam and Eve's original sins. But no problem. Jesus, you see, died for your sins, and at baptism wiped the slate clean." With her finger, she blackens out a little spot. "This is your first sin." They're big on sin and punishment. Then, with the eraser, she blackens out a little more. "You've sinned again against God." Soon, more stains appear until black swallows all the white. "And if you die with all your sins, you go to hell. Saint Peter shuts heaven's gate in your face when you knock."

Later in Rome years later, we got as far as the Piazza Venezia where the later King Victor Emmanuele II, also sits on horseback. Braved the traffic across the piazza and saw more sights. Italians sure do drive funny. Pedestrians cross at will without looking. Curious nobody gets killed. But scary.

By then we were hungry and stopped off an Italian restaurant. The waitress took one look at us and directed to our seats – In Spanish. *"Por aqui, por favor.'*

"Sto molto emocionale de sta qui, al centro di la civilizacione e io voglio parlare itsaliano, per favore." (I'm very emotional being here at the center of civilization and wish to speak Italian, please). I mixed my Pimsleur's *Italian in Ten Days* with a little Spanish. We did, after all still speak the same Latin language at the time of Julius Caesar.

""Perche?" the waitress asks. Why?

"Perche quando en Roma, fache come le Romani." (When in Rome, do as the Romans do.")

She laughed and brought us our pasta and a meat dish. No vino, though. I'm a beer and rum drinker and I ordered a beer and a coke for Martha. After this very long day, we returned to the hotel to sleep. Got up early and the next day headed out early after a good breakfast.

Looking for Campo di Fiori and the Market, tried my Italian again. "Scuzi," I ask a woman. *"Dove il Campo Fiori, per favore?*

She seems puzzle. The Italians are nice and don't laugh at clumsy foreigners.

Another man explains we're far. We take a cab. See the market. More statues at the piazza Navonni. I swear the whole place is an outdoor museum. "Did the Trevi Fountain and threw in some coins. Sat on the Spanish Steps, but first ate at the MacDonald's next door, the cheapest place anywhere in the world – the people's restaurant. Visited the poet John Keats's house. It's a hobby of mine, visiting places where poets hanged out. The Pantheon was cool. Painter Rafael lies here. Victor Emmanuel, too.

We sign up for a tour of the catacombs outside the city. The mini bus takes us down the Via Apia, the old Appian Way that traversed the entire ancient empire. Went down into the tombs where a nice Irish priest conducted the tour. That's where they buried early Christians. Saw where the martyred St. Cecilia rests and a few skulls.

"And if you die with all your sins, you go to hell. Saint Peter shuts heaven's gate in your face when you knock," I again recall those nuns. Serious stuff, indeed, I think, cowering in fear, vowing to go to mass Sundays, not eat meat on Friday, or disobey my mother less I burn to a crisp in that terrible place awaiting sinners. And if I stumble, I make it a point to show up at confessions Saturdays to wipe the slate clean, unloading my transgressions on a good Irish priest. "Go, me lad - before Jesus on his cross, and his mother the Virgin," he whispers in the dark confessional. "Ten Our Fathers and ten Hail Mary's." Of course, I succumb to White Castle burgers the very next Friday, skip mass on hot days and hop the Six train, then the 12 bus, to Orchard beach, careful of course not to go in too deep less I drown – then burn. Back to confession the following Saturday to again ask the good Irish priests for absolution, never denied, if I again kneel before Him and his mom. The cycle begins again, though I grow anxious less He return to earth suddenly, and that final trumpet catches me off guard

Learned all about the Hebrew children, too, Moses, Isaiah and the rest of them.

"Jerusalem is no more."

We missed the tour bus back and walked back on the Via Apia, dodging lots of cars that have now replaced those ancient chariots, hugging the wall lining the road. Scary. We got change at a store and took a city bus back.

Saw the spot where St. Peter tried *running away from the persecuting Romans. The spot where he runs into Jesus, a cross in his arms." Domine, Quo Vadis?"* Where are you headed, Lord?"

"Back there to be crucified again. You've failed me, Peter."

Embarrassed, Peter goes back and is crucified. Upside down, as he's not worthy to die like the Lord." Made me think about how I, too, ran away from my religion. "And if you die with all your sins, you go to Hell. Saint Peter shuts heaven's gate in your face when you knock." Though I no longer believe everything those good Irish priests taught me, this religious instruction made me, if not a saint, a generally moral, if flawed human being. I was moved by the church that now stands there on the Via Apia. We didn't go in, as we saw enough churched to last us a lifetime. And in all of them, and forever on the cross the Savior poses eternally, his tired face at once in agony and in bliss. Blood flows from the palms and feet nailed to the cross and from below his crown of thorns. And through the many stained-glass windows decorated with the lives of the saints, the sunshine flows and illuminates the churches.

Saw the Vatican that same day. Must say, these Popes lived a good life. The Sistine Chapel is something else. But the Body of Pope John 23 blew me away. He was Pope when I made my first communion. They've preserved it and he lies in a glass tomb visible to all.

Saw Nero's home, the Domus Aurea -or what little remains of this fabulous temple his ego built. Nero destroyed a great deal of Rome to build it, while it's said he played his fiddle. Vanity, all is vanity. Bumped off his mother and many others. Burned a lot of Christians to light his home at night. Not a nice man.

We picked up our Trafalgar tour and headed out to see the rest of Italy. But instead of reporting for our orientation meeting in our hotel, we took a tour outside Rome. Trevi Gardens, built by Renaissance Cardinal with all the nickels and dimes collected from poor peasants. Vanity, all is vanity. Saw the Emperor Hadrian's Villa, too. Vanity, all is vanity. Marx was right to an extent. Sooner or later, the bourgeoisie had to take these people out. Then working-class people, the Proletariat, had to take them out, too. Our tour guide Ermano, who's face is now blurred in my memory, didn't like it and resented us for the rest of the tour. But after all, he wasn't paying us – we were paying Trafalgar and him. We did another walk around the Forum before we left for the rest of Italy. I corrected him on the succession of Roman emperors. After Nero committed suicide, Ermano said Vespasian became top dog. I interrupted and explained the generals Galba, Otho and Vitellius ruled very briefly in the years 68 and 69 B.C. Ermano's frown lives forever in my memory, though, all I remember of him. He ignored me, and went on to list other rulers.

In Pisa, first stop after Rome on the tour, black hawkers yelling in Italian, Spanish, but mostly in English, greeted our tour bus. "Welcome to Africa," Ermano, said sarcastically. I peg him for a racist of sorts. The population is down and the birth rate decreasing, Italy needs people from elsewhere to do the menial stuff. And Italians resent them. Ermano 's resentment written on his face I also remember. What Italians need to do is start making babies again.

The Tower does lean, though some English engineers have worked out something to stop it from tilting more. Other towers have toppled over – or been toppled by invaders. Perhaps Italians have a racial memory of this past and perhaps it's why they resent, fear, or plain dislike immigrants.

Here Galileo disproved an ancient theory of Aristotle that falling objects fall at different speed, according to their mass, the heavier falling faster. Aristotle found no need to empirically bear this out, his reason sufficient to make this conclusion. Galileo performed a scientific experiment with a cannon and a smaller object thrown out a window on the top of the tower, to test this hypothesis. I performed it in physics class with Dr. Goldsmith in my college days in Oswego. Forget the objects we used. Gold ball and a lighter object? Or a heavier object? A tennis ball. Time their descent. Both fell at the same speed.

This is called scientific empiricism. Reason is very important, but true knowledge comes through observing through our senses. Sight. Touch. Smell. Hearing. Taste. And always measuring. And this intellectual churning of ideal begins in Italy during the Renaissance. Galileo with his telescope proved the sun and not the earth is at the center of the universe. The church put him under house arrest. See, in Exodus, Joshua orders the sun to stand still and so Galileo went against its dogma. It's all an optical illusion. A lot of the bible is illusion.

"George, George, why do you persecute me?"

'I don't persecute you, Lord. It's just that my own views evolved throughout junior and senior high school."

-I mastered biology with Mrs. Barth, who sent us to the Museum of Natural history during Easter break, 1965 to research evolution. Human evolution became one of my greatest loves. Later after high school history, biology, and chemistry came college geology, anthropology, mythology and more art classes. Learned about other religions – not all of them believing in Jesus or the Virgin. Later while teaching Global at the Bronx High School of Science, I needed to teach the world's religions to my students. Judaism which begat not only Christianity, but Islam as well. Read parts of the Koran. Hinduism. And Buddhism. I'd once gone chanting with a friend. I was objective, laying out the basic beliefs of all and having my students, not me, judge the relative merits – and demerits– of each.

I'd heard about Darwin and in the Bronx Zoo studied those gorillas and chimps, not to mention those hominids in the Museum of Natural History. Adam? Eve? Hmn. Read about the Greek god Dionysus who died and was reborn every spring – right around our Easter. Oh my God? Could it be *Him*? Read Plato's *Republic*, the part about this not being the real world, just a shadow of the real world up there somewhere. So that's where our heaven came from. And why did those statues of the Virgin Mary look so much like Venus and Athena?

Could the good nuns and priest have gotten it all wrong?

We were late getting back to the bus and Ermano drove off and nearly left us. Perhaps it was just a warning to be on time for departures. Or perhaps it was a resentment for not attending his orientation and showing him up with the business of the Roman emperors.

Drove through the western coast, by passing many pretty cities seen in the distance. Recco. Portofino. Rapallo.

By passed Genoa, too. It's a modern, ugly, industrialized town. But it's said to be the home of a guy named Columbus. Though he was born Crisoforo Colombo, he renamed himself Colon. I'm very proud of the name Colon I share with the Admiral of the Ocean Seas, Cristobal Colon – not Columbus, as the English- speaking world renamed him. He sailed under the Spanish flag, despite Italians marching up and down Fifth Avenue on October 12th. I fancy I may descend from the Admiral of the Ocean Seas himself, father of two sons, Diego and Luis Colon, big players during the early settlement of Puerto Rico. Maybe. Maybe not. I'm going to look into that, too someday, maybe even take a DNA test. By the way, in 1453, the Turks conquered Constantinople and renamed it Istanbul. That set-in motion the Italian decline as it curtailed commerce with the east. It's why Colon needed to find a new passage to the west. Make no mistake the Italian city states did go into decline, and Italy became just "geographical expression" for a long time after that.

Ermano was beside himself when I ran this all down to our tour group. "You know," he told the group, "It's like saying Shakespeare wasn't really English, but that he went somewhere else to write his plays." Bull shit, I thought. It's a stupid analogy. But I said nothing, fearing he'd throw us off the bus. Though I'd sue later, in the meantime I'd be in a bind. Felt like kicking his ass at that point, but Jail was not an option, as it was for Saint Paul.

Turin is very European, more like Paris than Rome or Florence. And it's kind of dirty With down to earth people, like the guy drinking beer in a park. Usual Roman gate. The arcades are nice. And of course, there's the Duomo di San Giovanni - or Church of Saint John - adjoins the Royal Palace of

Turin (just so) by way of the Chapel of the Holy Shroud, the Sacred Shroud of Turin. Saw a replica. "Sorry, Jesus, but it's not really you looking at me. It's a forgery."

By the way, I dropped some acid later in life and altered my state of consciousness. Sorry, but that dude - John of Revelations – was tripping, too and hallucinated on the island of Patmos, which I saw later. Nah. Jesus isn't coming back – dead people don't – not even nice Jewish rabbis after 2,000 years. And why should He after what He got last time he came?

Not to say it's not all going to end – maybe soon. Yes, there's a comet headed this way. The dinosaurs couldn't help it. But at least, they were too smart to have organized religion. We can. At least, they didn't burn anybody at the stake or engage in holy jihads. Yes, the ice caps are melting. Fire? I've no desire. Ice? That won't be nice. Will we blow ourselves up? Maybe. But John didn't really have a clue. Neither did the Mayans or Nostradamus.

Florence's museums, palaces, and churches and artistic treasures impress. The Cathedral, the Baptistry, the Uffizi, the Bargello. The Ponte Vecchio spans the Arno River. Michelangelo's David must be seen. My, what big hands you have, King of Israel. Slay Goliath! I need to write a book just on Florence. And a separate book on Venice. And Venice? What can one say about Venice in this short space? Gondolas, St. Mark's Church. Vivaldi's house. There's much more for a separate treatment. But must mention the palace of the Doges. Bridge of Sighs. And the paintings of the Battle of Lepanto, where the European powers let by the Italian city states got together to stop Turkish expansion. It was Italy's last hurrah. I said nothing to Ermano. Of Verona, there's Juliet's balcony. "Romeo, Romeo, wherefore art thou Romeo." In Bologna, I had the best meal of my life. But I didn't come across Jesus in those places.

In Mantua, there's the church with the blood of Jesus, brought back by the Roman soldier who stuck his sword while Jesus was on the cross. I would never do such a thing.

Milan has a lot. But of course, the big attraction is the Last Supper, complete with Judas who Jesus says will betray him. I'm no Judas, just a rational empiricist

Assisi was last stop on the tour. After a lunch of lasagna, salad and ice cream, we went to the Basilica did San Francesco. I'm wearing shorts. Would they let me in? Saint Francis wouldn't have had a problem. Neither should anybody else. Nobody does. We go in. there's Giotto's painting of the saint's sermon to the birds.   Rich, worldly Francis hears God's call after a stint as a soldier. Captured and ransomed, he cast off his riches and takes a vow of poverty and does well. We see his tomb. Wow, there he is. Come back, Francis, come back to our modern age of material and corporate greed and teach us how to live. "George, George, why do you persecute and betray me?"

No, Jesus, I don't persecute or betray you. So yes, I read the Koran. Flirted with the Enlightened One. Sorry Mohammed. Sorry, Enlightened one. Jesus is still my guy. Yes, Jesus, you're my guy. You took a drink at the last supper and at that wedding at Cana, cracked opened the kegs with your holy powers. Take a nip myself, from time to time. You never packed a sword – I've never packed a gun. No, I won't sprout wings when I go. But neither will I burn to a crisp, though our indiscretions do burn us at times.

No, the priests and nuns didn't get it wrong - just some of the minor details. I honor those Hebrew prophets, too, especially Isaiah. "Undo the heavy burden – let the oppressed go free," I always say. And although I haven't shed all my material possessions like Saint Francis they're not important to me.

I do on to others as I wish they would do unto me. Try to turn the other cheek, though not always successfully. I turned the other cheek, shook Ermano's hand at the airport and gave him a good tip.

No, no Lord, I don't persecute you. Just telling it like it is. It's all about leading a good life, as I have - generally speaking, of course. Taught the children of the Bronx about books and how to write. Taught a daughter to do right. When I book, I'll live on in them.

Their memory will be my heaven.

CHAPTER TEN

Israel (2010)

More religion

Went to Israel – *and* back. Incredible. Walked through the Old and New Testaments and saw places first visited in bible class in my old South Bronx parish, St. Athanasius, as filtered through the good Irish priests and nuns there. But in Israel I realized religion is not really about sin and punishment and hell.

After connecting at Frankfurt, an El Al flight took me to Ben Gurion Airport in Tel Aviv with my wife Martha (You've met her before), her mother Ana and my sister- in-law Rosa. I'm mostly leaving them out of this account and I'll just tell you I translated for them as after many years in America from Ecuador, they have not yet mastered English. Perhaps we'll do a Spanish language tour, if I even bring them again. I explained the sights and refreshed their knowledge of the Bible. But so as not to offend women readers with female "stereotypes, I'll mention them only rarely. A Trafalgar (English language) Tours operator drove us to Jerusalem. The Israeli landscape, though varied, lacks color, in a land the size of New Jersey. My memory paints it a drab brown broken in places by palm trees, olive groves and rare green. It has beaches, blue beaches, especially along the Mediterranean side in Tel Aviv and environs. Deserts, of course. The Negev. There are seas, lakes and rivers. And yes, mountains. The St. Athanasius priests and nuns got its geography right. We stayed in a hotel in the New Jerusalem, quaint, but modern. With Macdonald's, Kentucky Fried Chicken and Pizza huts, it's accumulated many of the sins of the new era. Among them, next to millennium old structures, hastily constructed - abodes built to accommodate Jews fleeing the holocaust. They don't help. Art Decco buildings do. Before picking up the tour, we did Old Jerusalem by ourselves. Not to be believed - like walking in 4 B.C. when King Herod rebuilt Solomon's Temple – though it must have seemed less seamy then. Arab peddlers line its narrow, grimy alleys, hawking their wares, competing with food vendors peddling here. All that's left of the temple is the Wailing Wall after war and destructive waste through the millennia.

At Saint Athanasius fifty years ago, a nun dressed in black, bonnet on her head, takes the eraser and dusts out a white, round circle on the blackboard. "This is your soul at birth, pure and clean," the good sister explains "Well, not exactly," she continues," because we inherited Adam and Eve's original sins. But no problem. Jesus, you see, died for your sins, and at baptism wiped the slate clean." With her finger, she blackens out a little spot. "This is your first sin." They're big on sin and punishment. Then, with the eraser, she blackens out a little more. "You've sinned again against God." Soon, more stains appear until black swallows all the white. "And if you die with all your sins, you go to hell. Saint Peter shuts heaven's gate in your face when you knock."

Serious stuff, indeed, I think, cowering in fear, vowing to go to mass Sundays, not eat meat on Friday, or disobey my mother less I burn to a crisp in that terrible place awaiting sinners. And if I stumble, I make it a point to show up at confessions Saturdays to wipe the slate clean, unloading my transgressions on a good Irish priest. "Go, me lad – before Jesus on his cross, and his mother the Virgin," he whispers in the dark confessional. "Ten Our Fathers and ten Hail Mary's." I kneel in front of the cross and recite the prescribed penance for my sins. Of course, I succumb to White Castle burgers the very next Friday, skip mass on hot days and hop the six train, then the 12 bus, to Orchard beach, careful of course not to go in too deep less I drown – then burn. Back to confession the following Saturday to again ask the good Irish priests for absolution, never denied, if I again kneel before Him and his mom. The cycle begins again, though I- grow anxious less He return to earth suddenly and that final trumpet catches me off guard.

A tingle of emotion flowed through my fingers touching the Wailing Wall – like touching King Solomon himself, imbibing his wisdom through my fingers. His temple is long lost to age – and war – and all that's left is this old retaining wall. Its main section of the wall, meleke limestone, measures about 187 feet (57 m) long. Its stones average 4,000 pounds, though the enormous Western Stone, weighs more than 1.1 million pounds (more than 500,000 kg). Twenty-eight stone layers lie above the ground and 17 below, with an underground tunnel running along the length of the wall.

I donned a paper yarmulke, picked up a pencil and paper, like the yarmulke, provided by some super orthodox tourist people in long locks, beards and black hats. Wrote a letter to God and left it in a crevice on the Wailing Wall. It's said to be his mail box. Asked Him for a long life for my grandson Ryan who was born the following month. Other Orthodox Jews in prayer shawls with prayer books, bowed and gyrated while reciting Talmudic passages in front of the wall, touching the wall, with one hand, prayer book in the other. Males only on one side; women on the other side. It felt like a home coming as I grew up across the street from a South Bronx Synagogue and at times flipped the light switch for my Jewish neighbors, as practice forbade them to work on the Saturday Sabbath. In Bible class, I learned all about the Hebrew children, too, Moses, Isaiah and the rest of them.

In this divided land one of Israeli sentries in drab olive uniform stopped me at the entrance to the Dome of the Rock. It's said the Prophet Mohamed ascended into heaven here at this famous mosque. Long before that, it's said the Patriarch Abraham attempted to sacrifice his son Isaac before God stopped him.

"Are you Moslem?" the Israeli soldier asked.

"No."

He shook his head. "Only Moslems can enter."

Religion scares me. Scares me a *lot*. Though there's no war right now, those guns hotel guards openly carry gave me pause. They've had lots of wars there. Israelites, Canaanites, Philistines, Assyrians, Babylonians, Persians, Greeks, Romans, Arabs, Crusaders, Turks, English. They've all killed themselves here. We picked up our tour and met our guide, Yahudah. Knowledgeable. Dark bearded, spots of white dotting his black hair. Very temperamental. Went to Jericho, called Megiddo, where it's said the Apocalypse will begin. Its strategic location at the crossroads of the biblical world led the armies of the Middle East to maneuver there at one point or another. Today, only stones remain, reconfigured by Israeli archeologists. and architects.

When I re- entered Israel from the West Bank, a machine gun toting Israeli soldier in a yarmulke entered the bus with an unsmiling female companion in matching drab olive uniform. No, it wasn't a machine gun. It was a mini Canon. Her eyes scanned the passengers and landed on mine. Only on mine. I was the darkest one there.

"Passport?"

I think she pegged me a Palestinian terrorist sneaking into Israel.

"It's in my suitcase."

"ID?"

My New York State driving licensed satisfied her.

Scary.

Bethlehem, on the West bank in Palestinian territory. Easter Sunday, 2010. The state Department has issued a warning about travel to Bethlehem. But as we'd come this far, we had to go.

The Church of the Nativity sits atop, a hill, its grotto, or cave forms the base of the church and is associated with the cave where Jesus was born in a manger. Here, angels and Sheppard's sang in the adjoining garden and here came the Magi, according to tradition. It's designed is the typical Roman basilica, with five aisles formed by <u>Corinthian columns</u> and an <u>apse</u> in the eastern end, where awaits the <u>sanctuary</u>. Golden <u>mosaics</u> decorate its decayed walls. <u>Edward IV of England</u> donated its wooden rafters and lead to cover the roof, melted later by Ottoman Turks for ammunition against <u>Venice</u>. Winding stairways on either side of the Sanctuary lead down to Grotto (Wikipedia).

A 14-pointed silver star on the marble floor surrounded by silver lamps marks the exact spot of the manger. A white altar draped in lush red curtains is there. I rubbed a handkerchief on the spot and gave it to my daughter Iliana to give to Ryan my first grandson. The <u>Greek Orthodox Patriarchate of Jerusalem</u> maintains the sanctuary and church, but Armenian Christians, and Catholic priests have a say. At times they come to blows and the Israeli army must end these quarrels.

In April 2002, during the second Intifada, those interminable conflicts between Palestinians and Jews, some 50 armed Palestinians wanted by the <u>Israel Defense Forces</u> (IDF) locked themselves in the church with some 200 monks and other Palestinians who arrived at the site for different reasons. Because of the historic value of the building the IDF did not break into the building, but instead prevented the entry of food. The siege lasted 39 days and some of the gunmen were shot by IDF snipers. After lengthy negotiations it was agreed that the remaining gunmen would be evacuated to <u>Gaza</u>, <u>Spain</u> and <u>Italy</u>.

Yes, religion scares me.

Bethlehem, on the West bank in Palestinian territory. Easter Sunday, 2010. The state Department has issued a warning about travel to Bethlehem. But as we'd come this far, we had to go.

As my Trafalgar tour group reached the small opening into the grotto, the crowd, no mob, clawed and scratched itself into the little chapel where Christ was born. A fat Russian Orthodox tour guide stuck an elbow perilously close to my face so her tour group could go first, as if it were the Ukraine.

Yahudah the tour director ordered me to push back. "Punch her if you have to. Don't let them in!" But the baby born there 2,000 years ago later said something about turning the other cheek. It hardly seemed the venue for that. I no longer believe *everything* in the bible, but still believe *some*. People screamed and cursed. I stepped aside and let those Russians through first, then was the last one down. I kneeled in front of the where the manger stood.

Later, in Egypt, we'd see the spot where Joseph and Mary and the baby passed, fleeing an anxious King Herod who ordered young innocent newborn killed, fearing the one said to be a king.

Followed in Jesus' footsteps. The sights in Nazareth. Home of Joseph and Mary. The church of the Annunciation where Mary got wind she'd bear the Messiah. The River Jordan where John the Baptist dipped Jesus' head. Wife Martha dipped her feet, as did her sister Rosa and her mother Ana. We watched others being baptized by immersion as John immersed Jesus. I dipped my fingers but not my feet, as a diabetic, I don't wet my feet unless I have a towel and foot powder at the ready. But I did deep wade into the Sea of Galilee where He performed the miracle of the loaves and fish, next to a Kibbutz where we spent the night. Saw the Apostle Peter's house. "I will make you a fisher of men." Floated on the Dead Sea. Bought a bottle of wine in Canaan where He multiplied the wine at that wedding. Cesaria and Masada. The Crusader places where Christianity battled Islam. But most memorable proved Easter Sunday, 2010, back in Old Jerusalem. Stood in the Garden of Gethsemane where Romans came for Jesus. Peter jumped to his defense and sliced off one of the Roman guard's ear. Jesus picked it up, placed back where it belonged and healed this soldier.

That's what Christianity is all about.

Our guide Yahudah took us down the Via Dolorosa – and the Stations of the Cross. Here, Pontius Pilot condemns Jesus after the crowd wanted Barabbas freed instead. There someone wipes his sweat and blood. This impression on this wall is where He places his hand.

Simon takes his cross and carries it.

Black Eritrean Coptic pilgrims from Africa in white robes walk parallel to us towards Calvary. They mostly ignore us. My sister –in-law Rosa keeps studying the stands, looking at merchandize. I fear she'll get lost, stop, and urge her to keep up. They do kidnap people around here. Yahudah has already scolded her for buying from Palestinians and Rosa resents it. I soothe. I explain. Pogroms, The holocaust. Wars in

1948, 1956, 1967, and 1973.The Jewish – Arab animosity. I understand both points of view. And finally, late in the afternoon, we reach the Church of the Holy Sepulcher. It's a gray structure in Romanesque Baroque style. Inside await wonders. The cave from which Jesus arose. His anointing stone. The prison that holds him and the two thieves. Yahudah points to another spot. "Here, Adam and Eve are buried. I laughed in his face in disbelief. Now really. He frowned and gave me a dirty look...

But the first stop of course is where Golgotha is said to have stood. Here, atop a mound, wait three crosses on a stage like hill festooned with flowers and ornaments. One climbs up long steps. The pushing and shoving begins anew. Those black pilgrim Christian Copts surge past us. Two black Eritrean women held up precariously by walking sticks, both pushing ninety, push by me.

"Stick out your elbow." Yahudah says. "Trip them. Don't let them through." Yes, the world still out Herods Herod.

I refused, and not just because they reminded me so much of my grandmother Laura (died 1958). Went over to one of those African women who had trouble ascending the steps. She'd fallen behind the other pilgrims.

My Grandmother, *Abuela* Laura still lives in my heart and memory, a lovely, dark woman, always smiling, with black hair straightened with an iron comb common in those days, her eyes filled with purpose and determination. She holds a bible in most photos. She worshiped in a Pentecostal storefront church and once a week I accompanied her. Abuela visited St. Athanasius Church at times with a neighbor who tried to win her back for Catholicism. "I will enter wherever the Lord is present," she proclaimed, but remained a Pentecostal. She treated Jews and blacks courteously and they reciprocated her kindnesses.

A neighbor named Julie met a Japanese boy named Mickey she later dumped. Mickey popped in often and knocked hard on the Garcia's door. "Julie! Julie!" But it never opened. Japanese weren't popular after World War II.

Once night, Mickey came bearing the usual gifts and again performed his knocking ritual, pleading, crying, then kicking and banging, and in his fury, tried smashing down the door. "Julie! Julie! Open!" When it finally did, the whole family rushed out and began beating the hapless lover. Abuela came out, bible in hand. "Stop beating this man," she commanded. They did. She turned to the bruised Mickey on the floor and lifted him up. "She no love you," she gently placed a hand on his head. "You go now," she told him in limited English. "The rest of you go inside," she ordered his tormentors. They went inside. "He's God's creature and shouldn't be abused." He left never to return.

Though I no longer believe all of it, my grandmother and the priests and nuns made me a generally moral, if flawed human being. But I'm no saint, so don't call me one.

My own views evolved throughout junior and senior high school.

I mastered biology and human evolution became passion. Passed chemistry and physics. Studied history, geology, anthropology. And mythology. Learned about other religions – not all of them believing in Jesus or the Virgin. While teaching Global Studies I covered the world's religions to my students. Judaism which begat not only Christianity, but Islam as well. Read parts of the Koran. Looked into Hinduism and Buddha. But by then I'd heard of Darwin and in the Bronx Zoo studied gorillas and chimps, and those hominids in the Museum of Natural History. Adam? Eve? Hmn.

Read about the Greek god Dionysus who died and was reborn every spring – right around our Easter. Oh my God? Could it be *Him*? Read Plato's *Republic*, the part about this not being the real world, just a shadow of the real world up there somewhere. So that's where our heaven came from. And why did those statues of the Virgin Mary look so much like Venus and Athena? Is Mount Olympus the model of sorts for heaven? Read about Constantine and Roman politics. Could the good nuns and priest have gotten it all wrong? Read the Koran. Flirted with the Enlightened One. Even checked out the Pentecostals. Puerto Rican Pentecostals – especially Puerto Rican Pentecostal girls

So, did Jesus really rise? Is He really coming back? I don't know. I do know he never carried a sword and I never carried a gun. Sorry Mohamed, sorry Buddha. Jesus is still my guy. Sorry Lord if I no longer believe it all. If you didn't want me to think, then you shouldn't have given me a brain and the use of reason.

Stepped aside and let those old African women through. Took the one that resembled my grandmother by the hand and lifted her up. I swear it was like I was seeing my *Abuelita* again after she long ago went to her rest. Led her up those stairs. We were the last ones up where three crosses mark the spot where Jesus died with the two thieves. We made the sign of the cross. We prayed. This is Christianity. And the rest? Still honor those Hebrew prophets. Especially Isaiah:

"They shall turn swords into plowshares.
Spears into pruning hooks...'
Nation shall not raise sword against nation..."

Wish everybody would honor him, too.

I recalled Mark Twain's quips in his *The Tragedy of Puddenhead Wilson*. "The problem with Christianity is it ain't never really been practiced." Wrong. I practiced it in Israel. I've practiced it in life. I still practice it though not as well as I should. If there's really a heaven please let me into heaven. A lot of white still shows on the blackboard of my soul.

CHAPTER ELEVEN

Russia (2008)

On Marxism and Classless Societies

Leaving Finland, we headed for Russia through the Karelian Forest, peaceful and bucolic, its pleasant greenery, trees and tranquility un shattered as at times by innumerable Russo-Finnish wars. At the border crossing that morning our tour group marveled at an endless fleet of trucks waiting to cross into Russia from all over Europe. The Russians remain paranoid about their border and male guards in drab olive uniforms with red stripes and stars on their caps inspected each one. The Russians' long, bloody history accounts for this paranoia. Customs proved interesting.

We got there post Communism and I asked myself throughout our stay there, "Why did Communism fail?

A.fat, poker faced female guard in a drab, olive uniform took our passports. She looked at me up and down, then studied the passport and visa pasted in it, examined them again, eyed me again, then the passport with visa again, then me again and again without smiling. She finally stamped it, still unsmiling, and waved me through. My wife Martha underwent this same scrutiny behind me before waved through. She observed the other smile less fat female border agents.

"Why are they so fat, these women?" Martha asked.

"They're preparing for the next famine," I surmised. "Famine crosses at times the Russian border." Meanwhile, more male soldiers, also in drab olive uniform lead a menacing German Sheppard through our bus. The dog sniffs our luggage and the bus.

First stop, Vyborg, a quaint town once part of Finland and changing hands frequently these past centuries. We first saw dreary Soviet style apartments in the outskirts of the city that remind one of New York City projects, with less charm, factories in disrepair, but then nice buildings from Finnish days. Pretty lakes and a renovated Russian Orthodox Church with characteristic onion dome, brighten up the scene. Religion has re-entered Russian life after the official atheism of the now defunct communism. But two replicas of Viking ships in a small lake steal the scene. Vikings ruled Russia back in the days when the Slavs around the 800's A.D, called on Rurik, Viking leader of North Jutland, to protect them from other invaders. Called the Rus, they stayed, founding the Kievan Dynasty, ruling from the city of Kiev and giving the country its name.

We stopped at a restaurant for lunch. Décor clean and acceptable. Russian black bread. Borsch soup. Bah. I hate cold soup. Ice cream. Coffee. Black. Terrible. Service decent. Waitresses did smile. Then we hit the hard, at places unpaved rocky road to St. Petersburg. Russian roads are bad. But what do you expect of a communist state? They've rediscovered capitalism, but the old timers miss the old "From the womb to the tomb" notions that Marxism preached. There are no more free rides whereby the state takes care of you. Will it be for the better?

We reached St. Petersburg.

Yes, St. Petersburg. Peter's city, Peter the Great.

Before we get into why Communism failed, let's examine why it came about. It begins with the Czar rulers of Russia. Peter is a good place to start. Peter ordered poor serfs to toil and create an instant window to the West facing the Baltic sea, wanting in the 18th century to modernize Russia, moving it away from its eastern, oriental, Slavic past into the future. He himself toured Holland, France, England incognito, gathering modern scientific knowledge and shedding old superstitions and an over reliance on religion. Peter ordered his city built on the sea and created a fleet of war ships to compete with European navies and fight his wars against the Swedes.

In his poem "The Bronze Horseman," the great Russian poet Alexander Pushkin writes of Peter...

On a deserted, wave-swept shore,

He stood – in his mind great thoughts grow –

And gazed afar. The northern river

Sped on its wide course him before;

One humble skiff cut the waves' silver.

On banks of mosses and wet grass

Black huts were dotted there by chance –

The miserable Finn's abode;

The wood unknown to the rays

Of the dull sun, by clouds stowed,

Hummed all around. And he thought so:

'The Swede from here will be frightened;

Here a great city will be wrought

To spite our neighborhood conceited.

From here by Nature we're destined

To cut a door to Europe wide,

To step with a strong foot by waters.

Here, by the new for them sea-paths,

Ships of all flags will come to us –

And on all seas our great feast opens.'

The city was renamed Petrograd in 1914 to remove its German name at the beginning of World War I. Then, it was changed to Leningrad before its name once again reverted to St. Petersburg when communism ended.

We finally got there and it's a beautiful city – once you leave its outskirts and see its inner old city on the River Neva. Here he ordered his nobles to shave their beards and build their palaces on its waterfront and canals. His presence is all over his city, atop equestrian statues, always ready atop his steeds leading Russia forward, his 18th century tri cornered hat atop his head. His houses and monuments are everywhere. Especially the Peterhaus, with the summer palace and the Hermitage, one of the great sights.

The ship Aurora greeted us on the shores of the Baltic where it sits as it did that fateful day in 1917 to signal the beginning of the Russian Revolution. Those peasants and workers rose against the tyranny of Peter's Romanov successors. Later, in the palaces of the later czars, I'd understand, san the history books, why there was a Russian Revolution in 1917. But for now, the first night, we took a dinner cruise with music while I admired those charming homes along the Neva. It evokes Amsterdam, and has something of Bruges in Belgium with its architecture and brownish waters. But it's not Venice. Venice is Venice. Magical, the ride down the Neva, made more magical still by an ample supply of vodka and Russian pink champagne. Dressed up in Russian garb by the musicians who gave me a balaclava guitar, I strung it and sang, though can't remember whether in English or Spanish. Or was it Russian magically acquired? Food good. Caviar of course, and other dishes. Can't remember the menu. No Borsch. Yak!

First, the Fortress of Peter and Paul, built originally to defend the city, but used as a To house political prisoners. Here Peter murdered his son who conspired against him. Here also the writer Dostoyevsky was imprisoned. Next, we saw the Church of the Spilled Blood, so named for Jesus' blood, but also to commemorate 1883's assassination of Czar Alexander III. It boasts those onion like structures on top. We saw the statue of Michael I in a square where the Decembrists conspirators rose against the Tsars in 825 only to be quickly suppressed. The hawkers were everywhere peddling their wares.

That second night we caught a folklore show. Can't imagine how they can do those steps. Puerto Rican, I think are the best dancers in the world, but those Russians are pretty good, too. We waited in line to get in behind some Chinese tourists who bought Russian dolls from street hawkers. Examining one, I saw it was made in China and chuckled at the irony. We later caught a ballet, Swan song, after a dinner. Caviar is an acquired taste I never quite acquired, but did like again, the vodka and champagne. Ballet is also a taste I never quite acquire. Martha loved it. I found it boring.

We strolled down Nevsky Prospect, the main thorough fare of St. Petersburg, examining its great shops and sights. After a spaghetti and meat ball lunch at a Sbarro, we took pictures at the statue of the poet Pushkin in a park. Born in Moscow in 1799 into Russian nobility, Alexander Pushkin's great grandfather had been an African brought from central Africa to serve as a page for Peter the Great's daughter. Devoted to social reform, he was banished for a time from Russia proper, although later pardoned and returned. Always touchy about his honor, he fought thirty-seven duels, losing his last one to a French officer in the Czar's guard, who Pushkin accused of trying to seduce his wife Natalya Pushkina.

CHAPTER ELEVEN

Russia (2008)

On Marxism and Classless Societies

While we studied then another Russian Orthodox Cathedral, a dark, Gypsy kid followed us, begging for money. There all over Europe and they've followed us around in Spain, especially in Seville, where they tried to con us with sleight of hand. In Florence, they also nagged and harassed, and in Bologna where one tried snatching a fellow tour group woman's pocket book. In Paris, outside the Pompadour Museum of Modern Art, they also hassled us. But here in Russia they sure seemed out of place. I have no prejudices against any race of people – except for gypsies. They brag about their inherent evil and claim to have stolen the nails from the cross.

"Nyet. Nyet! Nyet! Nyet! Nyet!" I kept yelling. But the little mother fucker wouldn't take Nyet for an answer and grabbed at my pants, trying to put his hand in my pocket, before I pushed him away. Nearly kicked his fucking ass. Waved my fist at him and he finally went away. Glad no policeman showed up. The tour guide warned us that the police are even worse than gypsies and often shake tourists down for money.

Went by bus the next day down the Street of Strikes. On the way to the town of Puskhin Cstares, named after the poet. Saw a statue of the chemist Mendeleev in front of the house where he classified the elements. A large colorful replica of the Periodic Table adorns the building. Nearby Pavlov conditioned his dogs. In a square there is a statue of, <u>Sergey Kirov</u>, the popular communist leader of Leningrad and enemy of Stalin, who assassinated him, and led to the great purge by that paranoid dictator. No statues of Stalin remain in this great city.

Outside the city there is a great memorial to the defenders of Leningrad, as this city was once called, who held back the German armies of Adolf Hitler for three long years. In the Russian cold they held out against starvation and constant bombardment, but never capitulated. Neither did the two other "Hero Cities" of Moscow, Stalingrad, Sevastopol Make no mistake about it, it was Ivan Ivanovich, the poor Russian soldier, and the Russian people themselves who bore the brunt of that epic struggle against the evil forces of the Nazis. A million inhabitants of Leningrad died in the struggle.

But St. Petersburg for to me has always been about the Russian Revolution. Tens of thousands of conscripted serfs died building his city. Among Peter's vanities is his Peterhof, his great palace built to rival that of Versailles. Many of the great monarchs of Europe tried emulating Versailles. Though nothing remains on the inside, the grounds outside are a rich splendor of fountains, statues and garden facing the Baltic Sea. We took pictures of everything, including the grand stairway.

Then, there is the grand Summer Palace of the Czars, which we reached after a bus ride to the city of Pushkin Cstares, named after the poet Pushkin who studied there. Catharine the Great commissioned it built in the Rococo style and her daughter, the Empress Elizabeth expanded it. It's magnificent façade of white and blue and gold. Real gold. The inside boasts the Stasov staircase, the Portrait room and others before entering the great Amber Room, we took off our shoes and were given soft slippers so as not to scratch the floors. The Empress Elizabeth, didn't wear the same dress twice. While the poor workers and peasants toiled, the Czar lived in splendor. Tolstoy's serfs. Chekov's serfs.

Then there is the Winter Palace, now the Hermitage Museum, one of the world's great art museums, boasting great works acquired by Catherine, who built it and here, after bumping off her husband and cavorting with her many lovers.

Selfish Czars.

Something had to give. Yes, Marx was right about certain things. Yes, history is in a sense a series of class struggles. In 1825, revolutionaries rose in what's called the Decembrist Movement, quickly suppressed. Later that century, the revolutionaries assassinated Czar Alexander III In 1905 there was an uprising, quickly suppressed. Then the last Czar Nicholas II went on his stupid war against the Japanese and lost, setting in motion a series of events that led to the 1917 Revolution, not the least World War I which Nicholas entered in support of his fellow Slavs, the Serbs, against the Slavs traditional enemy, the Germanic Prussians and Austrians. More misery for the Russian people.

The last Czar, Nicholas and his German wife, the last Empress Alexandra, luxuriated here with their four daughters and the heir to the throne, the hemophiliac Tsaravich Alexis. After years of interbreeding, this disease appeared as a curse to the royal Romanovs. It's been trace to a gene in the English Queen Victoria, the ancestor of both Nicholas and Alexandra, distant cousins. Several wise men tried advising Nicholas – the great Stolypin, among them. Nicholas wouldn't listen.

The Empress Alexandra, despised as "the "German woman" by Russians, bought in the monk Rasputin to help. Another one of my associations with this city is in fact this mystic fraud with supposed healing powers. He gained the confidence of Alexandra after apparently curing the young Tsaravich, though how, it's not clear. Rasputin then came and went in the palace at will. A drunkard and sexual degenerate, it was rumored he slept with the empress. The Russian upper class despised and plotted to kill him. Rasputin supposedly told the empress that if anything happened to him, the house of the Romanov would come to an end.

The story goes that a nobleman named Felix Yusupov, married to a niece of the empress, invited Rasputin for drinks and a meeting with Yusop's wife. We visited the sumptuous Yusopov palace on the Neva River where it all came down. After feeding him cakes and wine laced with cyanide, Yusopov began to poison him. Rasputin, according to legend, wouldn't die, so at the end, Yusopov and an associate shot him and dumped his body into the Neva River. All kinds of legends have developed, among them that Rasputin wouldn't drown, and his body began to float on the river despite the poisons and the gunshots. But die he did.

And yes, the Revolution did come to Russia, and yes, the Romanov dynasty did come to an end. The great ship Aurora fired its guns to signal the start and hit the winter Palace. The last of the Royal family were executed by a revolutionary firing squad and their bodies hidden for a long time. Later, the bodies were found and reinterred in Saint Petersburg in the Peter and Paul Cathedral with the rest of the Romanov rulers since Peter the Great. We visited their tombs in a separate chapel there. - a very emotional experience.

But then communism also had its evil – at times worse than anything Ivan the Terrible or the Romanovs could dish out. First came the slaughter of the peasants clinging to private enterprise

Lenin could not stomach. Then came the monstrous gulags of the Stalin era and the mass deaths of many as Russia industrialized.

So again, communism doesn't work. Russia seems prosperous and westernized after giving up on communism and embracing capitalism, as have just about all the former socialist countries except Cuba. No, communism doesn't work. Even Fidel Castro has said so. Capitalism, for all its evils does. Human beings, like all animals in the natural world, have a pecking order and classless societies don't exist. Marx said, "From each according to his ability, to each according to his need." But again, human beings strive to better themselves and rise socially and economically – if need be, at the expense of others. That's part of nature, too.

Twenty-five years before Glasnost and Perestroika, Mrs. Miller, my ninth grade social studies teacher in Junior High School 45 in the Bronx rendered the best explanation yet on the difference between communism and capitalism. "Let's say George here is a doctor," she said, pointing at me. "He has no children and has studied long and hard to become a doctor. "Then she pointed at Frank Ercalno. "And let's say Frank here is a shoe maker with seven children. So, who gets more help from the government? Frank the show maker does because he has more of a need. 'From each according to his ability, to each according to his need.' So why should you sacrifice and work hard if you're not going to be rewarded for your effort?" That lesson has always stayed with me.

I taught it to my students when I taught Global at the Bronx High School of Science. And then one day, while at Bronx Science, we received a visitor from the Soviet Union, a Russian school principal from a school in Moscow with which we had an exchange program. I noticed his terrible teeth. Actually, they weren't teeth, but plates of metal replacing the teeth he'd lost. That's what dentistry is like in a communist society. He took out a pouch of tobacco and rolled a cigarette. "May I try one of yours?" I said, offering him a Marlboro, which he declined. He rolled up one for me and I lit it and it was the most god-awful thing I've ever smoked. Again, that's what cigarette makers produce in a communist society.

My brother-in-law served as a marine mechanic on the aircraft carrier Nimitz. One day, a Russian pilot defected to South Korea and his MIG fighter ended up on the Nimitz where my brother-in-law got a chance to inspect it. "It was a piece of junk," he said. Yes, it flew and it could fire its weapon. But it was the shoddiest piece of construction my brother-in-law had ever seen. Communism goes against the grain of human nature. Like China and Eastern Europe, Russia is prosperous because it abandoned communism and went back to capitalism. It has its evils also.

But it's better than communism.

To conclude, the most singular memory of Russia is that Russians don't smile. The tour guides do and so earned good tips. But not the hotel clerks or the supermarket workers where we bought water and snacks. "Why don't they smile?" Martha asked.

"Because of the Russian past," I explained. Vikings. Mongols Turks. Ivan the Terrible. Bolsheviks. Stalin. Nazis."

Our main tour guide explained it best. "In Russia, they're always preparing and steeling them for the next Holocaust.

It was then on to Estonia.

CHAPTER ELEVEN

The Spain of my Ancestor

Been to many places, but first saw Spain in 1978, before England, or France, the rest of western Europe, part of the old Soviet empire, North Africa and China. First, I wanted to see *La Madre Patria* - the motherland of all Hispanic people. I experienced Madrid and Andalucía in the south. Went again in 2007, again to Madrid and the south, with brief forays into Portugal and Morocco. On this third time, I went north. But this account begins in Sevilla in the south, in Andalucía, the true soul of Spain, at the casket of my ancestor. I fancy him my ancestor, the central focus of this narrative. What remains of him lies in a casket in the massive cathedral of Seville, along with the crosses, statues of the Virgin Mary and other saints, laced with the gold and silver of the Americas taken from the Indies and my other ancestors – the Taino Indians of Puerto Rico.

The cathedral, like many in Spain, began as a Moorish Mosque during the Arab domination of Spain, then became a Catholic church after the Christian *Reconquista* that ousted these Moslems. Like irreverent English tourists, I tired of the many Spanish cathedrals. "ABC," they say. "Another bloody cathedral!" I repeat. I'll spare you a painting in words and just sketch its huge, imposing interior, in space enough for a stadium. Besides with crosses, the Virgins and other saints, there are the ever present left over Moorish trappings, mostly geometric patterns of design dictated by the Koran's strictures against depicting the human figure.

The casket rests on the shoulders of four life like statues representing Spain's historic regions: Castille, of course, Aragon Leon and Asturias. Cristobal Colon was his name. To Italians he's Cristoforo Colombo and it's even said he came from Genoa, Italy. Some make a case for Portugal, others for Poland and a few for Catalonia in Northern Spain, around Barcelona. He might even have been Jewish. But his origins form but interesting foot notes here. What's important is that he sailed for Spain and in her name united the world and won an empire. He spread Western Civilization to the New World – for better and for worse. Like me, he called himself Colon. He wrote in Spanish. I write in English. So, I'll call him, as we do in English - Christopher Columbus, Admiral of the Ocean Seas.

Colon was no saint, by our modern, politically correct standards. Yes, he brought about great evil and is vilified by revisionist historians and commentators. But I judge him in the context of his time. He, not the Vikings, Irish monks, the Chinese or the Japanese, united the continents, even if he never actually set foot on North America. The Indians never got around to inventing the wheel, had no horses to domesticate and never created a real alphabet, save for those Maya and Inca system of knots. Columbus, with his flaws – with his courage, intelligence and determination, spread this knowledge and technology Understand also the Indians didn't create a Utopia nor were they all that culturally advanced, for all their achievements.

Suffering from osteoporosis, like some of his relatives whose DNA confirmed that these are indeed his remains, few bones remain. In 1902, the body returned to Spain from Cuba, lost in 1898 to America, with Puerto Rico and the Philippines, after the Spanish American War. The Dominicans say he's buried in their capital, Santo Domingo, but. won't open the casket for genetic testing. On November 1st, 1493, Taino Indians of my native Puerto Rico, the second leg Of the tripod of my ancestry, greeted him – on his second voyage to the new world.

On my second voyage to Spain, I visited among other places, Salamanca, on the River Tormes, site of one of the great universities of the Middle Ages. Marvelous medieval structures decorate its plaza. The Spanish novelist Cervantes went to school there and left his initials carved into one of its desks... Another statue commemorates Lazarillo, protagonist of the picaresque novel *Lazarillo de Tormes*. It lies by the Tormes River, where Lazarillo is said to have been born. But it's the statue of Columbus and the sages that takes center stage. It commemorates Columbus' meeting with sages there, bouncing off them his ideas for a voyage west in search of China and India. He unfolds a map. One of the sages studies it. The others ponder his words. The Turks had earlier in 1453 taken Constantinople (Present Istanbul), blocking Western commerce with the east. Another outlet to the Indies was needed.

Columbus had presented his ideas to others, meeting with European monarchs - meeting with failure. The sages of Salamanca gave their consent. Soon, as every school boy knows, Queen Isabel of Castille, and her husband Ferdinand gave theirs - and money, ships and a crew for his voyage. But Rather than sell her jewels, Isabel and her husband borrowed from merchants and bankers, among them Spanish Jews.

The Re Conquest was over. It had begun in the north and in Burgos, at its cathedral, I saw the tomb of El Cid, whose exploits did much to retake parts of the south in the 800-year-old struggle against the Moors. By 1492, Toledo, Cordoba, Sevilla were long Christian. Earlier that year Granada fell, and with the fall, Christian domination was complete. Filled with a new sense of purpose, the monarchs felt God commanded them to spread the faith. Monetary gain from the trade with the east was also motivation.

But before Columbus got the final OK, he chased the Spanish monarchs all over Andalucia. Cordoba was an early and frequent stop. He met with them there in 1485 at the Alcazar fortress and at first turned him down. Besides the queen, another woman attracted him to Cordoba: Beatriz Enriquez de Harana, a weaver of humble origins. She would bare him a son. He'd visit with both several times after. In Cordoba's Alcazar, the fortress of the monarchs, on the banks of the Guadalquivir River. Ferdinand and Isabel prepared a final assault against Granada, the last Moorish stronghold. Its Mezquita became yet another Catholic Church. It's crosses and statues form but incidental decorations; the 856 multicolor arches supporting its ceiling forms its soul, lit up by light on their red and white stones I followed in Columbus' footsteps here in Cordoba, down narrow, winding, medieval alleys. He no doubt strolled down the Street of Flowers, stopping to chat at its many patios. Perhaps to speak of love to Beatriz.

Perhaps he wondered through the Jewish Section. La Juderia. No doubt he saw the Synagogue. But not the statue of Maimonides which appeared much later. And perhaps he wondered into the Plaza Judah Ha (levy). But that would've been, but long after this Jewish poet for whom it's named, here wrote verses. Wrote one was to wine. A guest at a home, he finds merriment and nice people. "But there is no wine," he laments. Verses to women. "Habib, habib," the females call to him. He responds. After a dissolute youth, he ultimately finds his God and to Him devotes his art and his life.

I read Judah Halevy with the pleasant Mr. Wiggins in Advanced Spanish in Dewitt Clinton High School – and other rounded out my grounding in Spanish literature with more sophisticated stuff. Medieval Romances in archaic Castillian. And even *Jarchas Mosarabes,* in the original, Arabic

– Hebrew dialect spoken by, among others, Jewish and Arabic poets like Judah Halevi. Jews and Arabs once upon a time lived in peace in Andalucia, Spain. The Jews, like the Moslems are long gone and with their exodus began Spain's decline.

With fall of Granada, the monarchs finally consented and received Columbus in the Alhambra Palace of the Moors. The Alhambra dazzles, free of Christian ornaments, with only arabesque designs of flowers and fruits and calligraphy as décor. There are fountains and gardens. And of course, pools of water. Washington Irving, American consul in Spain in the 19th century wrote *Tales of the Alhambra* and popularized it in the west. Columbus no doubt explored its narrow streets, may have climbed up to Sacromonte, and probably climbed through the Albayzin neighborhood.

As the Mexican composer Agustin Lara wrote…

"…Granada, your soil is filled with beautiful women, blood and sun."

But it was from near Seville that Columbus would sail, down the Guadalquivir River into the Atlantic and destiny. Seville, besides its cathedra, also has an Alcazar, where the monarchs received Columbus. Built by Arabs for Spanish kings, it has its Moorish and Christian trappings and many patios. In Seville, on my third trip, we stayed in the old Jewish section, in a hotel called the Jewish House (*La Casa de la Juderia*), a quaint old structure of wondrous mazes for hallways. The Maria Luisa Park was created in the 19th century and the Plaza Mayor didn't go up until 1929. Saw the bull ring and the tobacco factory where one Carmen, of opera legend, worked. Columbus didn't see them. But he no doubt visited also the old Jewish quarters, like he probably did in Cordoba, in Toledo and in Segovia. Like the Moors, the Jews also left their trappings. When the flow of gold from the Americas began, the Spaniards no longer needed them.

No, I won't bore you with yet another account of his meeting with the Indians and his other adventures. I did follow his footsteps in Santo Domingo where there's a large statue of him. Saw his last house in the new world. And yes, his body – maybe part of it – is said to lie there. There was disappointed he'd not reached India or China. But eventually he returned from Spain and again met with the monarchs, once, in Barcelona. There in the medieval maze of the Gothic section, an assassin tried to kill King Ferdinand. Barcelona is interesting. One rambles through Las Ramblas, a quaint commercial strip. One must see Gaudi's incredible La Sagrada Familia Cathedral, not just another bloody cathedral but an incredible surreal work of art. There's the seaport... Once, replicas of the Nina, the Pinta and the Santa Maria were displayed there. No more.

But a great statue of the Discoverer remains, pointing the way to the indies. So, no, he didn't find China or India. But he did find America for the rest of the world.

From my book: No, he (Columbus) was no saint, as modern, politically correct historians are too quick to point out.

Yes, he brought about great evil. Yes, he began the subjugation of my Taino and African ancestors. He bought disease – but inadvertently. Some like Genghis Khan did so deliberately, employing germ warfare to subdue and kill. Yet Columbus brought a third of my white Spanish ancestry. I won't disown him. We can't really judge him by our modern standards, any more than we can Genghis Khan. The human trail on this earth is soaked with blood. First, modern anatomically humans probably exterminated Neanderthals, intentionally no doubt, at first, but ultimately with superior cultural and material technology. Assyrians. Egyptians. The Greeks Alexander the Great unleashed. Certainly, Julius Caesar's Romans. All wiped out whole peoples. But each spread civilization. Hellenic. Roman. And less we forget, Napoleon, who despite his ferocity, did spread the ideals of the French Revolution. Liberte, Egalite and fraternite. I stand firm in my assertion he must still be judged in the context of his time. The Indians never got around to inventing the wheel, had no horses to domesticate and never created a real alphabet, not even those Maya system of knots. Columbus, with all his bad points, began bringing these essentials. Again, the Indians didn't exactly create a Utopia nor were they all that culturally advanced, for all their achievements.

Cortes was able to conquer the Aztecs quickly with a few men because the subject people the Aztecs brutalized joined him to undo the heavy yoke of these pre-Columbian imperialists, even if it's not politically correct to call them that. In his *Conquest of Mexico*, the Spanish chronicler, Bernal Diaz de Castillo relates how they cut off the hearts of their victims – while still alive- and heaped them on top of their pyramids as sacrifices to their gods. Cortes, though no saint either, finally ordered his men to put an end to it. The Incas were as brutal, not to mention the Iroquois in North America. If they killed less people, it's only because they lacked the technology to do so.

Was he Italian? Probably. But he sailed for Spain. The Indians took up bull fighting, not bocce ball and they now speak Spanish, not Italian. And when in 1453, the Turks conquered Constantinople and renamed it Istanbul they ironically, Columbus, set in motion the Italian decline as the Turks curtailed commerce with the east. It's why Colon needed to find a new passage to the west. Make no mistake the Italian city states did go into decline, and Italy became just "a geographical expression" for a long time after that.

So, was he my ancestor? I but fancy he may be my ancestor. Maybe. Maybe not. His sons Luis and Diego played *vital roles in Puerto Rico's early history. Maybe one day I'll take a DNA test. Maybe not. It's not all that important. But he is, along with Taino warriors and African slaves my cultural ancestor.

On one issue, however, there is no compromise – that nonsense that others discovered America. Did Vikings get here first? Yes. But do the Indians now worship Thor and Odin and read the Norse sagas in schools? No, they read Cervantes and Lope de Vega. Did the Irish monk Brendan the Bold get here first? Maybe. But did the Indians learn to drink Guinness Stout and play the Irish bagpipe? No. They drink Spanish wine and play the Spanish guitar. Now the Japanese did reach South America early and did play a role in the development of the Jomo – Valdivian culture of Ecuador, where my wife is from. But did the Indians become Sumo wrestlers, Samurai warriors and worship the emperor? No. The Chinese *may* have come here, but probably not. They had no real reason to come, as China was probably the greatest nation on earth, if Marco Polo is to be believed. During the Tang dynasty, they produced so much food, they had to burn a lot of it. Though a Chinese admiral did sail far, he turned back in Africa, as non-Chinese "barbarians" had nothing of value for the Chinese, but for a few animals he brought back as curiosities. In the improbable case some Chinese ship got blown off course, did the Indians become Confucian scholars, take up ancestor worship and acupuncture?

No, they became Roman Catholics.

That all these other folks came first form but interesting, though insignificant footnotes.

If I haven't yet bored you with my historic ramblings, please try the wonderful poem below. Sail on, sail on, and sail on. I mean, read on.

Columbus
Joaquin Miller

Behind him lay the gray Azores,
Behind the Gates of Hercules;
Before him not the ghost of shores,
Before him only shoreless seas.

The good mate said: "Now must we pray,

For lo! The very stars are gone.

Brave Admiral, speak, what shall I say?"

"Why, say, 'sail on! sail on! sail on!'"

"My men grow mutinous day by day;

My men grow ghastly wan and weak

The stout mate thought of home; a spray

Of salt wave washed his swarthy cheek.

"What shall I say, brave Admiral, say,

. If we sight naught but seas at dawn?"

"Why, you shall say at break of day,

'Sail on! Sail on! Sail on! And on!'"

They sailed and sailed, as winds might blow,

Until at last the blanched mate said,

"Why, now not even God would know

Should I and all my men fall dead.

The very winds forget their way,

For God from these dead seas is gone.

Now speak, brave Admiral, speak and say"-

He said: Sail on! Sail on! And on!"

They sailed. They sailed. Then spoke the mate:

This mad sea shows his teeth tonight.

He curls his lip, he lies in wait,

With lifted teeth, as if to bite!

Brave Admiral, say but one good word:

What shall we do when hope is gone?"

The words leapt like a leaping sword:

"Sail on! Sail on! Sail on! and on!

Then, pale and worn, he kept his deck,
And peered through darkness. Ah, that night
Of all dark nights! And then a speck-
A light! A light! A light! A light!
It grew, a starlit flag unfurled!
It grew to be Time's burst of dawn.
He gained a world; he gave that world
Its grandest lesson: "On! sail on!"

CHAPTER TWELVE

Istanbul and Turkey

Recovered Sick Man of Europe

D id the Greek isles, sailing east on a cruise ship from the port of P across the Aegean to the Bosporus and Black Sea all the way to Istanbul and Turkey. They're the same waters ancient Persian ships traveled from Turkey, as Anatolia formed part of their vast empire. They sailed the Hellespont in the other western direction to subdue the nascent democracy of the Greeks. The Greeks defeated the Persian menace and its notions of emperors as gods. I'd passed Sparta and the statue of its ancient king Leonidas. Passed close to Thermopylae where his 300 Spartans slowed down the Persian advance. Passing by Salamis and Marathon, where Byron treaded, my mind conjured up those ancient Greek ships sinking the Persian flee sent by Persian King Xerxes.

> The mountains look on Marathon—
> And Marathon looks on the sea;
> I dream'd that Greece might still be free;
> For standing on the Persians' grave,
> I could not deem myself a slave....
>
> And on that coast...

...Which looks o'er sea-born Salamis;

And ships, by thousands, lay below,

And men in nations; —all were his!

He counted them at break of day—

And when the sun set, where were they?

At the bottom of the sea. Western civilization stopped the encroachment of Asia and the East.

But this narrative begins much later at the Gates of Vienna – on <u>Septemb11</u>th, 1683.On that date Muslim armies commanded by the Turks of Anatolia, successors to the Persians farther east, took Constantinople in 1453. From there they continued the march of Islam throughout south east Europe were finally stopped at the Gates of Vienna by a man rarely mentioned these day, the savior of Europe and of Christianity, John III Sobieski. This good King, King of Poland and Lithuania, still a powerful kingdom at the time before its sad decline, led a coalition of Western troops against the Turkish leader Kara Mustafa, pressing the attack the next day until the Muslims retreated. Had Sobieski failed, Europe today might well be practicing Islam.

I visited his residence at Wilanow Castle in Warsaw and also his grave in Krakow back in 2005.

Since Mohammed founded the religion in the 600's AD, Christianity and Islam have at times engaged in a life and death struggle. Arab armies conquered Spain and would've continued into the rest of Europe had not another great hero, Charles Martell, the Hammer, stopped them in Tours, France in 732 – exactly 100 years after the death of Mohammed. Great Spanish heroes like El Cid drove them out of Spain in an 800-year struggle. Moslems would later triumph against medieval Crusader armies. The Turks became, after their conversion, the vanguard. Their conquest of Constantinople, renamed Istanbul, closed the oriental trade of Europeans with the Orient, creating the search for an alternate route that ultimately resulted in the discovery of America. The Turks were again stopped at sea in the great naval battle of Lepanto by a fleet commanded by Don Juan of Austria in 1571. There the Spanish writer Miguel de Cervantes, author of Don Quixote, the first great European novel, lost his left arm ("...For the greater glory of the right," he later wrote). The Turks continued their march, ruling a great deal of the Balkans and Greece, where the English poet Lord Byron lost his life fighting them for Greek freedom. They ruled Hungary and a good deal of Yugoslavia (Bosnia) and Southern Russia, where many still practice Islam.

In Rumania, Vlad the Impaler (Count Dracula) played a role in stopping them. Legend holds he would impale captured Turkish soldiers. No, not through the heart, but through the anus. Yes, they took it up the ass and the no nonsense Vlad lined them up in rows like so many scarecrows, maybe not scaring the crows, but the surviving Moslems. No, Vlad wasn't Mr. Nice Guy, but if the legend is true, it spared his homeland as The Turks seeing the fate of their fellow Moslems put Rumania BEHIND them and moved on. The Turkish Moslem armies continued their march until John Sobieski stopped them– on September 11th, 1683.

The rational, enlightened, empirical and scientific West had once again triumphed.

The Turks then went on a downward spiral, becoming the "Sick Man" of Europe and after a catastrophic defeat in World War I, lost all their colonies. They then embraced democracy, gave women rights and moved away from strict Islam, prospered and progressed, unlike their Moslem brethren not embracing modernity.

But long ago, in 1453, they had conquered Constantinople and renamed it Istanbul = a fabled city. There, I crossed into Asia for the first time, for Istanbul straddles two continents. First called Byzantium by the Greeks, the Roman Emperor Constantine created there a second capital, Rome itself not big enough to administer or a vast empire. He converted to Christianity and renamed re named the city Constantinople. It became very Christian, like him and its spiritual men spread the new, official religion in eastern Europe and the Balkans. But the city remained Greek, not Latin Roman, and later broke with the Western church. When barbarians overran the west, the Byzantine Empire survived – and thrived. Islam in the form of the Turkish Ottoman Empire, heirs to the ancient Persians, conquered it in 1493 and from there spread until stopped at the Gates of Vienna by John III Sobieski.

Crossing the Aegean from the Athenian Port of Pireus and the Greek Isles, the cruise ship reached the Dardanelles, the narrow passage that crosses into the Bosphorus waters through the Sea of Marmara and into the Black Sea. Modern Istanbul straddles both Europe and Asia. But before Istanbul, I got up at about 5 AM to behold Gallipoli. I'd drunk many Pina Coladas, danced and partied with Martha and two Miami Cubans we befriended on the trip. But I needed to get up and with fellow Australian travelers, gazed on Gallipoli. There in 1915, Turkish soldiers slaughtered many, many Aussies and Brits in their failed attempt to outflank the Turks and cut them off from their German and Austrian allies during World War I. It was perhaps the last glorious stand of the dying Ottoman empire. I saw fleetingly as the ship sailed by a great monument that commemorates this bloody battle. The Aussies snapped pictures as I took it all in with my mind's lenses.

But shortly after, Turkey lost it all – the Middle East, as well as the Balkans and their remaining middle eastern. possessions. General Mustafa Kemal lead this stand. Ataturk, as he became known, would transform Turkey after the war.

Istanbul is a magnificent city of mosques, palaces and other treasures. On the confluence of the Bosporus and the Sea of Marmara, the Sultan Ahmed Mosque, the Hagia Sophia, the Topkapi and Dolmahahhe Palaces appear in the panorama. There are modern buildings and the skyscrapers of the Levant main business district rival any in the world. Istanbul has a diverse industrial economy, producing commodities as varied as olive oil, tobacco, transport vehicles, and electronics.it has a modern finance center and a stock exchange.

But the old Mosque minarets seem to dominate the skies.

And the queen of its architecture is of course Haggia Sophia, constructed by the great Justinian I,in the 500's BC to the Virgin Mary, the central cathedral of the Eastern Orthodox Church. It boasts a magnificent dome and two large minarets reach into the skies. An elaborate fountain for the requisite ablutions before prayers lies outside. The Turks made it a mosque, of course, and at first hid Christian icons, But Haggia Sophia now functions as a museum and once again one can now see the mosaic of Justinian offering not only the church to the Virgin, but also the whole city. Other Christian mosaics of Jesus and the saints decorate it. It's classical Byzantine architecture with not only the mosaics, but marble pillars, a marble door and a vaulted nave.

Saw also the Blue Mosque. Fountains outside prepare with ablutions for the spiritual experience inside. Inside, an impressive geometric pattern dictated by the Koran's strictures against depicting the human figure for the main design. Multicolor arches supporting its ceiling forms its soul, lit up by light on their red and white stones. A none Moslem can enter here – after taking off his shoes. Not all mosques in other countries are open to non-Moslems.

The Turks have been most tolerant – up to now. Most are Muslim Turks, of course. But one sees many a white face, as their empire took in many southern Europeans. There are Kurds, of course, Greeks, Armenians and even Jews.

Prick got an attitude when we offered less money for two sets of postcards. Like Egypt. Hawkers all over the place.

We saw palace of the Ottoman Sultans. Topaki. Jewels and swords of gold. A lot of Jade. Most impressive are relics. Mohammed's foot prints and hair. A tooth. A letter he wrote. And of course, a sword. For it was by the sword that Islam was spread. Another sword of Abui Bakr, one of his earliest converts – and warriors. There's an armory. Turks took religious seriously and spread it with arms. Christianity did also. But those early apostles, like the Buddha and Jesus himself, were men of peace who promulgated their face through persuasion, not the. sword.

Didn't enter the harem, where one can see the reputed hand of John the Baptist. Wanted Turkish money. Guide said it wasn't worth it.

And of course, there's the Gran Bazaar. Magnificent array of spices, food, trinkets, clothes.

Outside the bazaar we waited for our guide with some Cubans we'd met on our cruise. We spoke in Spanish. This hawker tried to peddle some of his wares. "He made fun of my moustache. Called me "Mr. Vigote (Moustache) and implied I looked like a terrorist.

Asked where we were from – in Spanish.

My friends are Cubans from Miami. My wife, from Ecuador. Me, I'm from. Puerto Rico."

"Where? Caguas? Ponce? San Juan?

"Santurce, outside of San Juan."

He was not a professor of geography, but a common Turkish Joe. I figured he'd know San Juan, but not those other cities. Foreigners impress me always with their knowledge. And their linguistic abilities.

Ask people in the Bronx where Istanbul is. Good luck.

Conclusion

So, there you have it. End of my account. No France. No Mexico, Ecuador, Santo Domingo. No Eastern Europe. Back to the Bronx where I will stay. I've seen all I will probably see, but maybe they'll be more. Been in many places. But I always come back to the Bronx – my precioso el Bronx. So, do travel. Remember the world is a book. Those who don't travel read only the first chapter.